The
JOINT CHIEFS
of
STAFF

The
JOINT CHIEFS
of
STAFF

The First Twenty-five Years

LAWRENCE J. KORB

INDIANA UNIVERSITY PRESS • BLOOMINGTON & LONDON

Published in Canada by Fitzhenry & Whiteside Limited, Don Mills, Ontario

Manufactured in the United States of America

Library of Congress Cataloging in Publication Data
Korb, Lawrence J. 1939–
The Joint Chiefs of Staff.
Includes bibliographical references and index.
1. United States.   Joint Chiefs of Staff—History
I. Title.

UB223.K67   1976   353.6   75-16839
ISBN 0–255–33169–2   1 2 3 4 5 80 79 78 77 76

To the Memory of
Joseph A. Korb, Sr.

Contents

FIGURES AND TABLES

Preface

The Joint Chiefs of Staff is one of the most controversial bodies in the American political system. Yet it is probably one of the least understood. One author places the JCS on a par with the National Security Council in the decision-making process, while another feels that the JCS has as much impact in the policy process as does a group of cadets studying political science at West Point.[1] Individuals from every part of the political spectrum have denounced the JCS. Study groups and governmental commissions have found fault with the way it functions. Much of the criticism has been illfounded, however, because very few of the critics have been aware of the history and nature of the JCS.[2] How and why was it formed? When did it become an official body of the American political system? Who are the members and how are they chosen? What are the prerogatives and responsibilities of the Joint Chiefs?

This lack of understanding about the JCS is a result of at least two factors. First, the JCS is a relatively new structure within the American political system. It was not formally incorporated until 1947. Second, academic analysts have not paid very much attention to the JCS over the past twenty-five years.

During the 1950s there were many studies that dealt with the Department of Defense and the American military.[3] However, these analyses were on a macro level and thus did not focus on the JCS directly but treated it only peripherally. The literature of the early 1960s was concerned with the merits of the managerial innovations introduced into the Department of Defense by Robert McNamara.[4]

Once again the JCS was treated only indirectly. During the late 1960s and early 1970s, much of the writing on military affairs has been polemical in nature, condemning the militarization of American foreign policy[5] that resulted in the Vietnam War, or defending the military from being made scapegoats for the excesses of the "best and the brightest."[6] For the most part, these analyses have treated the JCS superficially, as symbols of the decadence of the military machine or of the frustration of the officers who were used by their civilian superiors. Many other analyses have shed a great deal of light upon the substance of national security policy, but few have told us very much about the Joint Chiefs of Staff.

This study will try to fill the gap. It will be concerned with the JCS as an entity. The first chapter analyzes the place of the JCS within the American political system and outlines the responsibilities and prerogatives of its members. Chapter two discusses the manner in which men come to the JCS, while the next two chapters look at the role that the Joint Chiefs have played in the policy-making process over the past quarter of a century. The final chapter projects the future course of the JCS. The focus of this study is not on the merits of such issues as the priority accorded to the area of national defense in American society over the past twenty-five years or the massive American involvement in Southeast Asia, but upon the role of the Joint Chiefs in making decisions about those issues.

The data for this study come primarily from the public record. Interviews with nine former members of the JCS and with several high officials in the Department of Defense were conducted to supplement the written record. None of those interviewed, however, is quoted directly in the text. Considerations of geography and time were the primary determining factors in the selection of interviewees. General Harold Johnson, United States Army, member of the JCS from 1964 to 1968, was the only official to refuse an interview. A partial list of those interviewed is appended to this study.

Although the final responsibility for what appears in the following pages is the author's alone, this book could not have been written without the encouragement and assistance of many people. I owe a particular debt of gratitude to Professors Michael Moss and Robert Rienow, my advisors at the State University of New York at Albany, to my colleagues of the Inter-university Seminar on the Armed Forces and Society and the Section of Military Studies of the International Studies Association, and to Commander Ronald Wells, the head of the Humanities Department at the U.S. Coast Guard Academy. A special note of thanks is given to my wife and children, who suffered patiently through the long months necessary to complete this manuscript.

The
JOINT CHIEFS
of
STAFF

★

CHAPTER ONE

An Overview

THE JCS TODAY

The Joint Chiefs of Staff (the Joint Chiefs, the Chiefs, or simply the JCS) is composed of four voting members: a chairman, who can be from any of the services; the Army Chief of Staff; the Chief of Naval Operations (CNO); and the Air Force Chief of Staff. The commandant of the Marine Corps is not a full-time voting member of the JCS because the Marines are part of the Navy Department. However, he does participate in meetings of the Joint Chiefs when matters pertaining to the Marine Corps are discussed. During wartime, when the Coast Guard would transfer from the Department of Transportation to the Department of Defense, the Chief of Naval Operations would represent the commandant of the Coast Guard at JCS meetings.

All of the members of the JCS, except the chairman, have dual responsibilities. In addition to being a member of the JCS, a chief has the responsibility for providing military direction to his service, although he is supposed to leave the actual running of the service to his vice-chief of staff and concentrate on JCS business.

In exercising their service responsibilities, the chiefs are subject to the authority of the service secretaries. Although a secretary has no legal control over the joint activities of his chief, the service chief is responsible for keeping the secretary of his military department fully informed on matters being considered or acted upon by the JCS. In the joint arena the Joint Chiefs are under the authority of the Secretary of Defense and the President.

Except in rare cases, the service secretaries play a very small part in the major areas of the service policy-making process. The initiatives and positions are developed by the service chief and his military staff, and the secretary usually contents himself with acting as a spokesman for these service positions. For example, the secretary usually has very little say in the preparation of his departmental budget. His actual function, as Wilber Brucker, Secretary of the Army from 1955 to 1961, so aptly stated, is to give it "three cheers and send it up the line"[1]—to the Office of the Secretary of Defense (OSD). Yet the secretary then defends the programs contained in his departmental budget with the assistant secretaries of defense, the Secretary of Defense, and the Congress. The service secretary does play a role in managing the department, in implementing and carrying out OSD or White House directives and decisions. However, to be effective in this role, the secretary must be regarded by his service as an advocate of its programs. Eugene Zuckert, Secretary of the Air Force from 1961 to 1965, supported the Air Force's poorly conceived B-70 program even though "the facts and logic belied the Air Force's position."[2] In the B-36 controversy, Francis Matthews, Secretary of the Navy from 1949 to 1951, was so far removed from the position of his officer corps that he was useless; he resigned from sheer embarrassment.[3]

Occasionally, a service secretary like Paul Nitze, Secretary of the Navy from 1963 to 1967, does play a major role in the policy-making process. However, Nitze, who was serving as Assistant Secretary of Defense for International Security Affairs for the three years prior to his Navy appointment, was a confidant of Secretary McNamara, a former director of the State Department's policy planning staff, and already playing a major role in the defense policy process.[4] It is not clear whether his position as Secretary of the Navy helped or hindered his effectiveness in the policy process. But for every Nitze there are several John Connallys and

Elvis Stahrs who resign from the service secretary post in a very short time out of sheer frustration.[5] It is interesting to note that Brucker and Zuckert, who recognized the limitations of the position, also spent the longest terms in office for their respective services. Brucker served for five and one-half years and Zuckert for four years and nine months in a position which normally sees a turnover every two years.

On joint matters the service secretary is even less involved. Air Force Chief of Staff John McConnell and the other members of the JCS knew that Air Force planes began bombing Cambodia secretly in 1969 and conducted 170,000 bombing sorties against this neutral country, but Air Force Secretary Robert Seamans did not, and, what was worse, he inadvertently misinformed Congress and the American people. Figure 1 depicts the organizational position of the JCS and the service chiefs within the Department of Defense as of 1975.

Figure 1: The Department of Defense, 1975

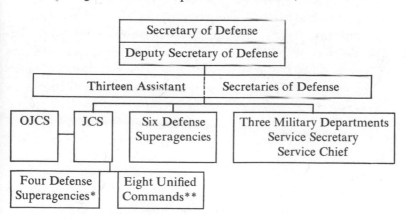

* Defense Communications Agency, Defense Intelligence Agency, Defense Mapping Agency, Defense Nuclear Agency
** Alaskan Command, Atlantic Command, Continental Air Defense Command, European Command, Pacific Command, Readiness Command, Southern Command, Strategic Air Command

The chairman of the Joint Chiefs of Staff is a member of one of the services, but during his tenure as chairman, he has no service responsibilities and outranks all of the active duty officers of the military services regardless of lineal position. Although the chairman can come from any military service, no Marines have been selected to date, nor are any likely to be in the future, because of the comparatively small size of the Corps; the Marines receive only 3 percent of the Defense Department budget.

There are no legal provisions that compel the President to rotate the position among the services. Eisenhower believed that such a practice was desirable, but Kennedy and Johnson appointed only Army officers to the post. With the appointments of Admiral Moorer and Air Force General George Brown as chairmen, Nixon appears to have reinstituted the rotation policy of his former boss. Even though the chairman has no service responsibilities, he has had nearly forty years of association with his branch of the armed forces, and few military leaders expect the chairman to shed his service orientation or parochial bias. For example, during the chairmanship of Admiral Moorer, the Navy received the largest share of the defense budget, while the Army fared better in the Johnson administration, when Taylor and Wheeler occupied the top spot. Therefore, most military officers agree with Eisenhower that the rotational policy is a good idea and would favor institutionalization of the practice. When Maxwell Taylor broke the rotation pattern by moving from the White House to succeed another Army general as chairman, he roused the ire of military officers of all the services.

Military officers are appointed to the JCS by the President with the advice and consent of the Senate. Since 1969, service chiefs receive a nonrenewable four-year appointment. The chairman is appointed for a two-year term and can be reappointed once, except during wartime. However, like other presidential appointees, all members of the JCS really serve at the pleasure of the President. Congress has never refused a presidential request to extend or renew the term of a chief beyond its statutory limit, nor have they ever acted to prevent the President from dismissing a chief before the end of the legal term. In addition, the Senate has never refused to approve a presidential appointment to the JCS.[6]

The major responsibilities, which are given to the JCS by legal statute,[7] may be grouped into four categories. First, the Joint Chiefs are the principal military advisors to the President, the National Security Council (NSC), the Secretary of Defense, and the Congress, and have direct access to all of these structures. Second, they prepare strategic and logistic plans that provide guidance for the development of the defense budget, military aid programs, industrial mobilization plans, research and development programs, and the contingency plans of the combat commands. Third, they review the plans, programs, and requirements of the separate services and unified commands. Fourth, the Joint Chiefs assist the President and the Secretary of Defense in the exercise of their command responsibilities. The second and third categories of JCS responsibilities, preparing and reviewing plans, are routine and need no further elaboration. However, the advisory and command functions are quite complex and often misunderstood.

The responsibility of being the principal military advisors within the executive branch is presently carried out primarily by the chairman through the National Security Council system as indicated in figure 2. The chairman of the JCS is one of the three statutory advisors to the Security Council itself and is a member of the six major subcommittees of the Council: the Washington Special Action Group, the Intelligence Committee, the Defense Program Review Committee, the Verification Panel, the Service Review Group, and the Undersecretaries Committee.[8]

Membership on the National Security Council or its subcommittees does not guarantee any military input into the decision-making process. Presidents Kennedy and Johnson did not use the Security Council to make foreign policy. Real policy decisions were made by ad hoc groups and sometimes then legitimated in the Council. President Nixon promised to reinvigorate the National

Figure 2: The National Security Council, 1975

National Security Council

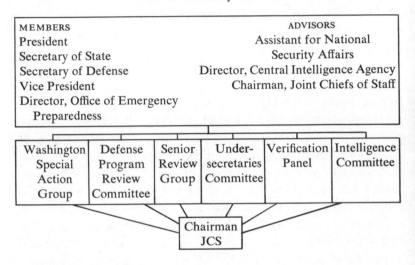

Security Council system, and in the early days of his administration he held frequent meetings of the Council at which policy was made. However, by the third year of Nixon's first term, policy making had drifted to the White House and Henry Kissinger's NSC staff. So closely did Kissinger's staff hold information on such critical issues as the SALT (Strategic Arms Limitation Talks) negotiations and the U.S. China policy, that documents were smuggled to the JCS by Kissinger's military liaison.

In many ways the position of the Joint Chiefs as advisors to the President paralleled that of the State Department. Both have statutory responsibilities to provide advice to the President, but from 1961 through 1973 that advice was not usually solicited until after the decisions had been made. Likewise, from the end of World War II through 1960, both the chairman of the Joint Chiefs and the Secretary of State were quite influential in the making of foreign policy. JCS Chairmen General Omar Bradley and Admiral

Arthur Radford were almost as close to Presidents Truman and Eisenhower as Secretaries of State Dean Acheson and John Foster Dulles. (Chapters three and four will discuss the changing role of the JCS in the policy process.)

In addition to the National Security Council system, the JCS is given access to the President in the yearly budget reviews. All of the postwar chief executives have allowed the JCS a "day in court," sometime in late December, to discuss the upcoming defense budget. Although these days in court usually come too late in the budget cycle to bring about major shifts in resource allocations for the next fiscal year, they have often laid the foundation for future fiscal year defense budgets. It was during these days in court with Lyndon Johnson that the chiefs made known their unhappiness with Robert McNamara's decision not to go ahead with deployment of the antiballistic missile (ABM). The first year President Johnson backed his secretary, but the following December he sided with the JCS and directed Secretary McNamara to announce an ABM deployment.

The JCS also briefs all incoming Presidents This usually occurs during the November-January transition phase, but when Vice-Presidents Johnson and Ford succeeded to the Presidency, it happened almost immediately after the takeover. The Joint Chiefs met with Lyndon Johnson on November 29, 1963, one week after John Kennedy's death and three days after his burial. The first JCS briefing of Gerald Ford took place on August 13, 1974, four days after Richard Nixon's resignation.

JCS inputs to the Secretary of Defense also come in two forms outside the National Security Council system. The Secretary of Defense usually attends one of the triweekly JCS meetings. This practice was begun by Secretary Thomas Gates in 1959 and has been continued by his four successors. The Joint Chiefs also send thousands of written opinions each year to the defense chief on various national security issues.

The JCS advises the legislative branch through annual committee appearances. The chairman and each service chief go before the Armed Services and Defense Appropriations committees with a prepared statement on our military posture and submit to committee interrogations annually. In addition, one or more of the chiefs appears regularly before such committees as Foreign Relations and Government Operations as well as before various congressional subcommittees concerned with aspects of national security policy.

In addition to the formalized channels of access discussed above, the Joint Chiefs use a number of informal means to present advice to civilian policymakers. In 1967 and 1968, Chairman Earl Wheeler was a regular attendee of Lyndon Johnson's Tuesday lunches, during which the President and his advisors formulated national security policy, especially with regard to Vietnam. Likewise, Wheeler's successor, Thomas Moorer, was invited to Henry Kissinger's Friday breakfasts with James Schlesinger. The chiefs also use their extensive social contacts with Congress and the press to plant questions and leak selected information. For example, Senator Wayne Morse's opposition to the Gulf of Tonkin resolution resulted from information supplied to him by the Navy. Likewise, in 1954, Chairman Arthur Radford let it be publicly known he favored American intervention in Indo-China. Finally, the JCS often makes use of the 39,000 military personnel serving with other government agencies to convey its opinions. In 1971, Secretary of the Treasury George Shultz persuaded Secretary of Defense Melvin Laird to accept a $2 billion reduction in the 1972 defense budget. The chiefs used the military liaison officers on Henry Kissinger's staff to make known their unhappiness, and Kissinger convinced President Nixon to overrule Shultz and Laird.

The right of direct access to the President and the Congress gives the Joint Chiefs a unique advantage over other advisors in the game of bureaucratic politics by which policies are determined in Washington. "Direct access" to the President makes it quite difficult for their immediate supervisor, the Secretary of Defense, to maintain complete control over the chiefs. For example, Admiral

Arleigh Burke used this prerogative to go over the head of Secretary of Defense Wilson to President Eisenhower and convince the President to overrule Wilson's decision not to draft men into the Navy. Similarly, their right to make Congress aware of any recommendations that they deem proper has allowed the Joint Chiefs to make "end runs" to Congress when they have lost battles within the executive branch. This prerogative of the JCS so infuriated President Eisenhower that he referred to it as legalized insubordination and attempted to have it taken away.[9] JCS recommendations to Congress have enabled the chiefs to receive funds for such executive-rejected programs as the B-70, the F-12A, and the ABM.

The command function is as complex as the advisory role. Theoretically the JCS is divorced from the operational realm; the chiefs do not have any troops assigned to them, nor do they have any command authority of their own. By law the chain of command goes from the President, as Commander in Chief, through the Secretary of Defense, whom many refer to as the deputy commander in chief, to one of the eight unified or specified commanders depicted in figure 1, who are of four-star rank and statutorially equal to and often senior to the Joint Chiefs of Staff.[10]

However, as principal military advisors to the President and Secretary of Defense, the Joint Chiefs are not separated from the operational realm; they do assist their civilian superiors in carrying out their command responsibilities. The chiefs often recommend strategy and tactics on their own initiative to their superiors, and the civilian commanders rarely make an operational decision without consulting the JCS. Moreover, the job of translating the general guidelines decided upon by the civilian hierarchy into specific orders to the unified commanders is usually left to the chiefs. But, since the chiefs have no command authority of their own, all JCS directives that require combat action or unit movements must be approved by the Secretary of Defense. The President can delegate his command responsibility to the Secretary of Defense or to the unified commanders but not to the Joint Chiefs of Staff. For example, the authorization for the secret bombing strikes into Cambodia in 1969 was signed by General Wheeler, the JCS chairman, but had to be initiated by Secretary of Defense Melvin Laird.[11]

It should also be noted that the chiefs keep in close contact with the unified commanders and guide the communications between the field and Washington. On more than one occasion, this guidance has colored the information furnished by the unified commanders and the type and timing of requests sent from the battlefield to support JCS positions. For example, during the Vietnam War the Joint Chiefs encouraged Westmoreland to request enough troops to support its position that the reserves should be mobilized.[12]

As indicated in figure 1, the JCS is assisted in the exercise of its corporate responsibilities by the Organization of the Joint Chiefs of Staff (OJCS) and by four defense agencies which report directly to the JCS. The OJCS is presently composed of about two thousand military and civilian personnel and is divided into two parts, the Joint Staff and the JCS staff organization. The Joint Staff cannot by law exceed four hundred military officers and is composed of equal numbers of officers from the three military departments, with the Marines being allotted 20 percent of the Navy complement.

The Joint Staff is headed by a director and is organized along conventional military staff lines: personnel, operations, logistics, plans and policy, and communications-electronics. The director is a three-star general officer appointed for a three-year term by the chairman of the Joint Chiefs with the approval of the Secretary of Defense and the other members of the JCS. Although there is no requirement to do so, the position has been rotated among the three services.[13] The Joint Staff performs all of the normal staff functions except intelligence, which is carried out for the JCS by the director of the Defense Intelligence Agency (DIA).

The staff organizations of the JCS are composed of about a thousand military officers and six hundred civilians. The first of these groups was started in August 1960 in order to assist the JCS in planning the employment of retaliatory weapons systems against general war targets. Presently there are four groups assisting the JCS on such matters as SALT and mutual balanced force reductions (MBFR), law of the sea, and automatic data processing. These groups are placed in a staff capacity to the JCS in order to circumvent the four-hundred-man limit placed on the Joint Staff by Congress.

Of the ten superagencies in the Department of Defense, four are under the control of the JCS; that is, their tasks are given by and they report through the JCS. They are the Defense Communications Agency, the Defense Intelligence Agency, the Defense Mapping Agency, and the Defense Nuclear Agency. The other six agencies report directly to the Secretary of Defense.

Each service chief has, in addition to the OJCS and the superagencies, which are supposed to assist him in the joint areas, his own staff of about 2,200 people. Although this staff exists to help the chief in running his service, it also does a great deal of work in the joint area. Every paper prepared by the Joint Staff must be cleared by the affected service staff, and the service chief is briefed for his triweekly JCS meetings not by the Joint Staff but by his own service staff.

Just as each service chief has a vice-chief of staff to assist him in fulfilling his service responsibilities, so he has an operations deputy to help him in the joint area. The operations deputies, or "Little Chiefs," are three-star officers from the chiefs' own services.[14] The director of the Joint Staff functions as the chairman's operations deputy. The director and the operations deputies also meet three times a week and handle much of the routine JCS business.

The present organization and functions of the JCS are a result of nearly three decades of actual operation, legislation, and administrative directives. It is only by examining the history of the JCS over the past thirty years that one can understand how it functions today.

AN ORGANIZATIONAL HISTORY

Although the separate military services are almost as old as the nation, the Joint Chiefs of Staff traces its beginnings only to World War II. Soon after American entry into that war, President Roosevelt and Prime Minister Churchill created the combined Chiefs of Staff to provide strategic direction to the U.S.–British war effort. The President then formed the U.S. Joint Chiefs of Staff as the American representatives to the combined Chiefs of Staff.

From this seemingly simple beginning as counterparts to the British on the combined Chiefs of Staff, the JCS almost immediately assumed the role of corporate leadership of the American military organization. Under the authority and responsibility of the President as Commander in Chief, the JCS undertook the coordination and strategic direction of the Army and Navy. It became in effect a supercabinet for President Roosevelt and often bypassed the service secretaries[15] (just as these men were bypassed during the secret bombing of Cambodia twenty-five years laer).

Initially the American JCS consisted of three men: the Army Chief of Staff, the Commanding General of the Army Air Forces, and the Commander in Chief of the U.S. Fleet and Chief of Naval Operations. Soon after the JCS assumed direction of the war, the Chief of Staff to the Commander in Chief of the Army and Navy, or the chairman of the JCS, was added to serve as a "go-between" with the President and the service chiefs. Throughout World War II, the JCS operated without a formal charter on the assumption that such a charter might inhibit the Joint Chiefs from doing what was necessary to win the war. In fact, the JCS owed its World War II existence and powers solely to letters exchanged by the service chiefs of the Army and Navy. So little were the chiefs inhibited from doing what they wanted that their chairman, Admiral Leahy, was later to state that for all practical purposes there were no checks upon the chiefs. They combined command and planning within themselves and maintained direct access to and the confidence of the President.

Because the United States won such an overwhelming victory in World War II, much credit was heaped upon the JCS system. Even President Truman, who was quite skeptical of the military and its procedures, was impressed by the World War II activities of the JCS. On one occasion Truman told Admiral Leahy, the wartime chairman of the Joint Chiefs, that if the Confederacy had had a military organization like the JCS, the South would have won the Civil War.[16]

However, the wartime success of the JCS was more apparent than real. During the war the chiefs reached agreement only by numerous compromises and after long delays. Moreover, coordination in material and administrative matters was incomplete and was largely forced upon the Joint Chiefs by circumstances arising from the war. The JCS functioned effectively as a strategic planning and direction agency only in the European theater from mid-1943 until May 1944. Before that time the chiefs were unable to agree on basic strategy in the light of the President's wishes. After May 1944, the JCS took a back seat to General Eisenhower's Supreme Headquarters of the Allied Expeditionary Force. Finally, the Joint Chiefs actually had very little to do with the Pacific war. For all intents and purposes, the Navy directed the Pacific campaigns.[17] Nevertheless, in spite of these World War II difficulties, all the postwar unification plans took the JCS as a *fait accompli*. No one apparently wanted to quarrel with success, and the only question that arose was the exact delineation of the powers of the JCS within the military establishment.

The National Security Act of 1947 (NSA), which established the National Security Council and created the Air Force as a separate military department, legitimized the Joint Chiefs of Staff by establishing it as a permanent organization within the national defense establishment and by providing it with a joint staff of a hundred officers. This act designated the Joint Chiefs as the principal military advisors to the President and the Secretary of Defense and gave them several general responsibilities and prerogatives.

The chiefs were directed to prepare joint strategic and logistic plans for the services and were given the authority to assign logistic responsibilities to the services, to establish unified commands, and to formulate training and educational policies for the armed services.

The National Security Act restricted membership on the JCS to the three chiefs of the military services, the Army Chief of Staff, the Chief of Naval Operations, and the Air Force Chief of Staff. The framers of the legislation felt that the Secretary of Defense could fulfill the role played by Chairman Leahy during World War II. The act provided that the members of the JCS would be appointed by the President with the advice and consent of the Senate for a two-year term and could be reappointed once.

Like most pieces of major legislation in the American political system, the National Security Act of 1947 was basically a compromise between diverse interests. Passage of the act involved reconciling the positions of those who wanted one strongly unified military department and those who insisted on keeping the military services separate. The compromise that emerged was in many ways analogous to the compromise that emerged from the American Constitutional Convention of 1787. The Department of Defense was not a unified structure, but in reality a federal system. The preexisting military services gave away only a portion of their powers to the Secretary of Defense and in effect retained all those powers not specifically conferred upon him.

In many ways, the JCS was the balancing force in this federal system. Its behavior would in large measure determine whether the Department of Defense would become a true union or merely a confederation. For, as an organization of service chiefs, the JCS represented the separate, potentially disunifying elements of the new military establishment. But, in its corporate capacity, the JCS embodied the joint or unified military interest.

Over the past twenty-five years there have been many complaints about the way in which the Joint Chiefs have functioned. These complaints can be broken down into three categories. First, their own service duties have prevented the chiefs from giving proper time and thought to JCS functions. Second, in the joint arena, the chiefs have been influenced too much by service particularism or aggrandizement. Third, the chiefs have been politicized by the party in power and thus became partisan rather than military spokesmen. These defects became apparent as early as 1948, and, in an attempt to remedy these problems, several changes in the structure and functions of the JCS have been made since 1947. These changes took the form of legislation in 1949, 1953, 1958, and 1967, while several other modifications were accomplished administratively. These alterations can be grouped into three categories, roughly corresponding to the problem areas.

First, the service and operational responsibilities of the chiefs have been diluted and the individual services themselves have been downgraded. The 1958 reorganization act directed the Joint Chiefs to delegate the running of their services to the vice-chiefs and to concentrate their energies on their joint responsibilities. Moreover, defense secretaries have used the authority of the 1958 act to transfer most of the service functions to the eight unified commands and the ten superagencies. The military departments retained only training and logistic responsibilities. Finally, the 1953 and 1958 reorganization acts transferred responsibility for the conduct of operations away from the Joint Chiefs and to the unified commanders.

Second, JCS capabilities in the joint arena have been strengthened. In 1949, the position of military chairman for the JCS was reinstituted. Initially he was not allowed to vote in JCS deliberations, but in 1958 he was given that prerogative. Since he has no service responsibilities, the chairman can devote his full time to his responsibilities of serving as the presiding officer of the JCS and acting as the liaison between the Joint Chiefs and the Secretary of Defense. In 1953, the size of the Joint Staff was increased from 100 to 210, and in 1958 it was enlarged to 400. Control over the Joint Staff was transferred from the JCS as a whole to the chairman, and the staff was directed to cooperate fully with the Office of the Secretary of Defense and thus to form a single staff for the Secretary of Defense.

Finally, in the early 1960s, program budgeting was introduced in the Department of Defense. This technique is intended to enable the chiefs to view the capabilities of the separate services in program packages and thus pinpoint the areas where weaknesses or overlapping exist.

Third, attempts were made to insulate the JCS from political pressures. In 1949 the right to speak out against administration policy before the Congress was legislatively sanctioned, and in 1967 the term of the service chiefs was lengthened from two to four years.

Although on paper these changes have been sweeping, in actual practice they have had very little impact upon the manner in which the Joint Chiefs have operated. The problem areas that existed in 1947 still persist a generation later. The complaints of Melvin Laird, the ninth Secretary of Defense, about the chiefs were strikingly similar to those of James Forrestal, the first Secretary of Defense.[18] The comments concerning the JCS of the President's Blue Ribbon Panel on Defense Organization in 1970 echo those of the first Hoover Commission of 1948.[19] There are four basic reasons why the modifications have not had the desired effect upon the JCS.

First, many of the innovations have been structurally unsound, for example, giving the chairman a vote in JCS deliberations, increasing the term of office of the service chiefs to four years, and directing the Joint Staff and Office of the Secretary of Defense to act as a single staff. The JCS is not the Supreme Court or the

Congress. It is only an advisory body. Hence it matters little whether a position carries by a 2 or 3 to 1 majority. What really matters is the quality of the position. Likewise, giving a fixed four-year term to a member of the JCS is sheer folly. The President can easily transfer the chief to another command or simply demand his resignation. When the bill to increase the term was being considered by the Congress, the sitting chiefs opposed it. They reasoned that once a chief lost the confidence of his civilian superiors, his effectiveness would be diminished regardless of the time he had remaining in office. Finally, directing the Joint Staff to cooperate with the Office of the Secretary of Defense to act as one staff for the secretary is totally unrealistic. The members of the Joint Staff from one service do not even cooperate fully with joint staffers from the other services. While on the Joint Staff, they are responsive primarily to the interests of their own service. To expect them to operate in unison with a civilian staff is asking too much.

Second, none of the changes has altered the power base or constituency of the service chief. He still relies for his support on his service and must be responsive to its needs. A chief who loses the confidence of his service cannot be an effective member of the JCS. In 1949 Admiral Louis Denfeld, the CNO, was forced to choose between the Navy's desire to build a new supercarrier in order to gain a place in the nation's strategic war plans and the Secretary of Defense's wish to save money by cancelling the carrier. When Denfeld selected the latter, he lost the confidence of and his ability to control the Navy. A "revolt of the admirals" was precipitated and Denfeld became the first member of the JCS to be fired.[20] No other chief has subsequently made a similar mistake.

Third, the services have subverted the intent of many of the basically sound changes. The chairman seeks approval from the service chiefs before appointing the director of the Joint Staff and has rotated the directorship among the services. The services have made the unified commands their own fiefdoms; for example, the position of Commander in Chief of the Pacific (CINCPAC) is held in trust for the Navy and the European Command is regarded as belonging to the Army. Even a powerful Secretary of Defense like Robert McNamara could not shake the Navy's grip on the Pacific. Moreover, the unified commanders usually look to their service counterparts on the JCS for guidance and always keep them informed of their every move. As chairman of the JCS, Maxwell Taylor was able to dictate nearly every move of General Paul Harkins, the Vietnam commander.[21] The services have not sent their best personnel to the Joint Staff, nor have they rewarded those who have ignored parochial considerations while wearing the "Purple Suit." The service chiefs still look to their own staffs rather than to the Joint Staff for guidance on their joint responsibilities. Finally, the chiefs quickly learned that systems analysis was not value free. If the problem was structured in a certain way, the service chief could use systems analysis to support his own parochial viewpoint. For example, Navy analysts have argued that the Soviet fleet is superior to that of the United States, while systems analysts in the Department of Defense, using different criteria, have judged the fleets comparable.

Fourth, the changes have dealt with the symptoms of the problems and not the causes. The problem of the service chief is not that he cannot divest himself of his service duties. The real problem is he does not want to. The man who spends nearly forty years as a follower in his service sees his appointment to the JCS as the opportunity to remake his service in his own image. He does not view it as an opportunity to serve as a principal military advisor to the President and the Secretary of Defense. Recently retired CNO Admiral Zumwalt was so engrossed in reshaping the Navy and so little concerned with his JCS responsibilities that he sometimes skipped JCS meetings. He felt that the chairman, Admiral Moorer, would safeguard the Navy position in the joint arena.[22] Given a choice between the chairmanship of the JCS or the position of service chief, most military officers would opt for the latter. Admiral Radford was keenly disappointed when President Eisenhower selected him to be chairman rather than CNO and spent much of his time as chairman trying to run the Navy.[23]

None of the changes have altered the format by which the JCS reaches decisions or the process by which men reach the JCS. The remainder of this chapter will deal with the internal procedures of the JCS, while chapter two will analyze the process by which men rise to the top of their service.

THE JCS IN ACTION[24]

The Joint Chiefs of Staff meet regularly on Monday, Wednesday, and Friday at 2:00 p.m. in a specially configured room, referred to as "the tank," just inside the mall entrance to the Pentagon. These meetings are closed to outsiders and no transcripts are made. Until 1959 not even the Secretary of Defense attended these meetings. In that year, Thomas Gates began to attend at least one of the weekly meetings and his successors have continued the practice. Except with McNamara, the Joint Chiefs have responded favorably to this practice. The chiefs resented McNamara's intrusion because they felt that he came looking for support for his positions rather than for advice from them.[25] All the secretaries, however, have met with the chiefs on a regular basis in their own office.

At each JCS meeting there is a fixed agenda for the chiefs to consider. The agenda items are supported by position papers prepared by the Joint Staff. Most of the items on the agenda are the result of requests from the White House, the Secretary of Defense, or one of the unified commands for a JCS position on a particular issue. A small percentage of the agenda items are generated internally by the chiefs or by part of their organization. Each year the JCS takes action on some 15,000 items, ranging from such insignificant questions as uniform design to such far-reaching problems as targets for nuclear weapons.

Not all of the problems referred to the JCS are acted upon by the assembled chiefs. In fact the Joint Chiefs act on only 2.8 percent of the papers processed in their name.[26] The operations deputies come together at 10:00 a.m. to review the day's agenda and by unanimous consent can approve items themselves. In addition, there are four other ways to remove items from the JCS agenda. First, papers with relatively short suspense dates can be approved by phone votes of service planners.[27] Second, papers submitted to service planners are considered approved at the end of seven days unless a dissenting memorandum is submitted. Third, the chairman may act for the JCS on those matters wherein time factors preclude formal consideration. Fourth, the chairman, the director of the Joint Staff, or the heads of the joint directorates (J-6 Personnel, or J-4, Logistics) may take action on those matters that fall clearly within guidelines previously established by the JCS. The only item that the Joint Chiefs insist on considering personally is a recommendation for the Medal of Honor.

The process by which a decision is made within the Organization of the Joint Chiefs of Staff is quite involved, and its outcome is usually the result of fierce bureaucratic infighting among the three services, each desiring to safeguard its vested interests. The process, known as the "flimsy-buff-green-red striped procedure,"[28] normally begins with a directive addressed to the chairman. The directives are usually in the form of a memorandum and indicate a date for the receipt of a reply. Upon receipt of a memorandum request, the secretary of the JCS (a one-star flag officer who works for the chairman) determines the action agency within the OJCS and establishes the due date for action. The due date established is based upon having the final paper ready for consideration by the JCS at two meetings before the time the report must be submitted to the requesting agency.

The directive is assigned to an action officer within the agency designated by the secretary of the JCS. This officer prepares a report on "flimsy paper" and forwards it to the service action officers for comment. After the service action officers have made their comments, they meet with the OJCS action officer to discuss the flimsy and make recommended changes. When the flimsy report is agreed to or reaches a point where the issues in doubt cannot be resolved, it is published on buff paper and circulated within the OJCS for formal concurrence or comment. Changes recommended by the agencies of the OJCS, if acceptable, are incorporated into the buff paper by means of a corrigendum. In the event that there is a divergent opinion within the OJCS on a buff paper which cannot be resolved between the agencies concerned, the matter is referred to the director of the Joint Staff for his determination. After his decision, the report is submitted to the service planners. If the service planners approve the buff, it is sent to the secretary of the JCS for preparation on green paper in a final format. If any service planner disagrees, he prepares a memorandum for the OJCS action agency stating the reason he cannot concur and recommending proposed changes. If these changes are acceptable to all concerned, they are incorporated into the buff. If they are not, the action agency calls a planners' meeting to resolve the issue. If the divergency still cannot be resolved, the dissenting service prepares a formal statement of nonconcurrence, which is attached to the green as a supportive document along with the action officer's opinion of the nonconcurrence. The green paper is then submitted to the operations deputies for their consideration. If the operations deputies cannot agree, or if they consider the subject of sufficient importance to require JCS approval, they forward the paper to the JCS for their consideration.

If the chiefs agree, they forward it to the requesting agency. If they do not, it is forwarded as a split decision with the views of the dissenting chief or chiefs appended. Once a position has been approved it is issued on "red striped" paper. The entire process generally takes about three weeks.

The Joint Chiefs agree unanimously on the great majority of issues on which they are asked to reach a decision. However, most of the issues are routine and the splits come on the crucial matters of budget ceilings, force levels, and strategy. In the first years of operation, split views among the Joint Chiefs were relatively common. However, in the mid-1960s, when these military leaders realized that a strong Secretary of Defense, Robert McNamara, was using these splits against them, the chiefs began to work out their differences among themselves, and since that time JCS splits have become fewer.[29] The Joint Chiefs of today realize that, in an atmosphere of hostility toward "things military," split decisions help neither the military nor their service. In the 1950s and early 1960s, a Bradley, Burke, Ridgway, or Taylor could dissent from his fellow chiefs and receive a sympathetic hearing in the Congress and from the media. These men were well known and the public was sympathetic toward increased defense spending. Dissension among today's less well known military leaders would be pointed to by congressmen and journalists as examples of military ineptness. The chiefs of today are no less parochial in terms of service orientation than their counterparts of yesterday. However, they know that they can best enhance their service position only by presenting a unified front to the outside world.

However, the unanimous opinions of the JCS are often of the least common denominator or cumulative variety. The flimsy-buff-green-red striped process is designed primarily to protect service positions. Consequently, at each step of the process, in order to please each of the services, the issue is usually watered down or "waffled" so that it becomes meaningless, or service positions are simply added together and labeled as a joint paper. The JCS has become so bogged down in the cumbersome process which is so concerned with protecting each chief's own service interests that it has become addicted to the status quo and has never been a source of innovation in the national security policy-making process. Policies such as containment, massive retaliation, flexible response,

Vietnamization, and détente have been developed with negligible input from the JCS. Lyndon Johnson once complained to Army Chief of Staff Harold Johnson that the JCS never gave him any solutions, answers, or even ideas to deal with Vietnam other than to continue with existing policies.[30]

Let us now turn to a consideration of the type of men who rise to the JCS and complete this analysis of why the chiefs act the way they do.

CHAPTER TWO

★

The Men

THE JCS AS A GROUP

As indicated in table 1,[1] in the quarter of a century from the passage of the National Security Act of 1947 through the summer of 1973, twenty-eight men were appointed to the Joint Chiefs of Staff by five Presidents. Six of these officers have served both as chief of their service and as chairman of the JCS. Twenty-one men have served only as service chief, and one man, Admiral Arthur Radford, has served only as chairman. Ten of the officers appointed to the JCS have been Army generals, another ten have been Navy admirals, while eight have been Air Force officers.

With the exceptions of General Vandenberg and Admiral Zumwalt, who were some months short of their fiftieth birthday at the time of appointment, the appointees to the JCS have been in their fifties at the time of their initial selection, with an average age of fifty-five years. Hoyt Vandenberg, at forty-nine years and three months, is the youngest man ever appointed to the JCS, while Lyman Lemnitzer, at fifty-eight years and ten months, has the distinction of being the oldest man to serve as a Chief of Staff.

Tenure on the JCS has varied from as little as seven months to as long as eight years. Carl Spaatz, the first Air Force Chief of Staff, was in office for the shortest time, while the honor of having

THE MEN [27

served on the JCS for the longest period of time belongs to Earl
Wheeler of the Army, who served under three presidents. Wheeler
was Army Chief of Staff for two years and chairman for another
six. Both Wheeler and Arleigh Burke, who spent six years as
Chief of Naval Operations, hold the record for the longest time
in one position. The average time on the JCS for all of the men
is a little less than four years. While their time in office has been
somewhat shorter than that of the average tenure of the post–
World War II Presidents, the chiefs' time in office far exceeds that
of their immediate superiors, the Secretary of Defense and the
service secretaries. During this same period, ten Secretaries of
Defense have spent an average of two years and six months in
office. Service secretaries have had an even more rapid turnover.
The average tenure of a post–World War II service secretary has
been two years and four months. Thus, in addition to having the
edge in expertise over their civilian superiors, the chiefs also
possess the advantages that come from longevity in a position.
Six chiefs have served with no less than four Secretaries of Defense and another four have worked under three. These two factors, military expertise and longevity in office, compound the
problems faced by civilian secretaries who wish to impose their
will on this military elite. As we shall see in subsequent chapters,
the JCS eventually "outlasted" Secretaries of Defense Forrestal
and McNamara in office and achieved policies to which these two
civilian secretaries were opposed.

The members of the JCS are fairly evenly distributed both
by state and by region. As is indicated in table 2, the twenty-eight
chiefs came from twenty states and no state has sent more than
three men to the JCS. Their regional distribution closely parallels
the population density of the various sections. The more populous
Northeast and Midwest have each contributed ten men, while the
less populous South and Far West have produced five and three
chiefs, respectively. Although there is no evidence to support any
connection between origin and subsequent behavior, this even

TABLE 1

The Joint Chiefs of Staff, 1947–1973

Name	Service	Age	Position	Term	Home State*
Creighton W. Abrams	USA	58	COS	1972–74	Massachusetts
George W. Anderson	USN	54	CNO	1961–63	New York
Omar N. Bradley	USA	55	COS	1948–49	Missouri
		56	CJCS	1949–53	
George S. Brown	USAF	55	COS	1973–74	Kansas
Arleigh A. Burke	USN	53	CNO	1955–61	Colorado
Robert B. Carney	USN	58	CNO	1953–55	Pennsylvania
J. Lawton Collins	USA	53	COS	1949–53	Louisiana
George H. Decker	USA	58	COS	1960–62	New York
Louis E. Denfeld	USN	55	CNO	1947–49	Minnesota
William M. Fechteler	USN	56	CNO	1951–53	Washington, D.C.
Harold K. Johnson	USA	52	COS	1964–68	North Dakota
Curtis E. Lemay	USAF	54	COS	1961–65	Ohio
Lyman L. Lemnitzer	USA	58	COS	1959–60	Pennsylvania
		60	CJCS	1960–62	
John P. McConnell	USAF	57	COS	1965–69	Arkansas
David L. McDonald	USN	56	CNO	1963–67	Georgia
Thomas H. Moorer	USN	55	CNO	1967–70	Alabama
		58	CJCS	1970–74	

28

TABLE 1 (*continued*)

Name	Service	Age	Position	Term	Home State*
Arthur W. Radford	USN	57	CJCS	1953–57	Iowa
Matthew B. Ridgway	USA	58	COS	1953–55	Massachusetts
John D. Ryan	USAF	53	COS	1969–73	Iowa
Forrest P. Sherman	USN	53	CNO	1949–51	Massachusetts
Carl Spaatz	USAF	56	COS	1947–48	Pennsylvania
Maxwell D. Taylor	USA	53	COS	1955–59	Missouri
		60	CJCS	1962–64	
Nathan F. Twining	USAF	56	COS	1953–57	Oregon
		60	CJCS	1957–60	
Hoyt S. Vandenberg	USAF	49	COS	1948–53	Wisconsin
William C. Westmoreland	USA	54	COS	1968–72	South Carolina
Earle G. Wheeler	USA	54	COS	1962–64	Washington, D.C.
		56	CJCS	1964–70	
Thomas D. White	USAF	55	COS	1957–61	Illinois
Elmo R. Zumwalt	USN	49	CNO	1970–74	California

* The State in which the individual graduated from high school.

TABLE 2

Regional Origins of the JCS

Northeast	Midwest	South	Far West
Abrams	Bradley	Collins	Burke
Anderson	Brown	McConnell	Twining
Carney	Denfeld	McDonald	Zumwalt
Decker	Johnson	Moorer	
Fechteler	Lemay	Westmoreland	
Lemnitzer	Radford		
Ridgway	Ryan		
Sherman	Taylor		
Spaatz	Vandenberg		
Wheeler	White		

distribution of the members of the JCS is somewhat surprising in view of previous studies on the origins of the officer corps which have found the South overrepresented in that group. For example, Morris Janowitz discovered that 30 percent of the officers in the armed forces in 1950 were from the South.[2]

Table 3 contains a list of appointees by administration. President Eisenhower, who served longer than any of the other Presidents in the past twenty-five years, appointed nine men to the JCS. President Truman, who made the initial appointments to the JCS, named seven officers. Lyndon Johnson named four men to the Joint Chiefs and promoted a Kennedy appointee, Earl Wheeler, from Chief of Staff to chairman. In his 1,000 days, John Kennedy also made four new appointments, and recalled to active duty Eisenhower's Army Chief of Staff, Maxwell Taylor, to be his chairman. In his first four years in office, Richard Nixon appointed four new men to the JCS and promoted Johnson appointee Thomas Moorer from CNO to chairman. Thus each postwar President has had the opportunity to make an ample number of selections to the Joint Chiefs of Staff, an average of about one

TABLE 3

Appointments to the JCS by Administration

Truman	Eisenhower	Kennedy	Johnson	Nixon
Bradley	Burke	Anderson	Johnson	Abrams
Collins	Carney	Lemay	McConnell	Brown
Denfeld	Decker	McDonald	Moorer	Moorer*
Fechteler	Lemnitzer	Taylor*	Westmoreland	Ryan
Sherman	Radford	Wheeler	Wheeler*	Zumwalt
Spaatz	Ridgway			
Vandenberg	Taylor			
	Twining			
	White			

* previously appointed by another administration.

appointment for each year in office. However, many of the appointments to the JCS have come near the end of presidential terms. For example, Lyndon Johnson made two appointments in his last year and Nixon three. Thus, the incoming President has normally spent his first few years in office working with military advisors selected by his predecessors, and, except for Eisenhower, who replaced the entire four men within his first six months in office, the Commanders in Chief have allowed the holdover chiefs to complete their full terms. Sixty-eight percent of the chiefs have served under more than one President.

Even when he is able to make an appointment to the JCS, the President's options are still constrained. His field of choice is usually limited to a few top men in each branch of the armed forces, whose promotion into this elite group is rigidly controlled by the individual service. Chief executives who have been inclined to go significantly below the normal zone to elevate an officer with whom they are acquainted personally or by reputation have usually been persuaded not to do so. For example, in 1962 President Kennedy's advisors talked him out of appointing to the JCS a then

47-year-old major general named Westmoreland, who had impressed the President during a visit to West Point. Likewise, in 1972 Richard Nixon was dissuaded by Pentagon officials from naming as Army Chief of Staff Brigadier General Alexander Haig. Haig had performed brilliantly as Henry Kissinger's deputy and had undertaken many difficult diplomatic missions for the President and Nixon was anxious to place him on the JCS. However, Haig was junior to 240 other Army generals!

Generally, the President is unacquainted either personally or by reputation with the men from whom he must make his selection. In 1963, President Kennedy selected David McDonald to succeed the troublesome George Anderson as CNO although he had never met McDonald and knew nothing of his policy positions. Moreover, even when a chief executive does not like the policy views of a potential chief, oftentimes he must select him as the "best of the worst." Thus, President Eisenhower was put into the position of having to place on the JCS General Maxwell Taylor, a man whose views on Eisenhower's policy of massive retaliation were completely opposed to his own. Likewise, John Kennedy's first appointment to the JCS was Curtis Lemay, who could hardly be considered sympathetic to the style or substance of the New Frontier, and whose opposition to the Kennedy strategy of flexible response was well known.

The service, through its absolute control over the promotion system, is responsible for placing the officer in the field from which chiefs are selected. Since 1915 advancement through the two-star or 0-8 level has been made by formal boards of military officers from the individual service. Occasionally political leaders may set some guidelines for the promotions, but the actual selection is left to military officers, who can easily circumvent these guidelines if they wish. For example, during his time in office, Secretary of Defense McNamara, in order to get less parochial general officers, stipulated that joint service was to be a prerequisite for flag selection. The services easily got around this guideline by so broadly interpreting the concept of joint service that the stipulation was meaningless. Civilian leaders who have tried to get involved in the selection process have met determined resistance from the military. Secretary of the Navy Francis Matthews tried to block the promotion of Arleigh Burke to rear admiral by attempting to remove his name from the list chosen by the promotion board. Burke not only was promoted to admiral but also became Chief of Naval Operations.

Three- and four-star appointments are not made by the formal selection boards used for the lower ranks. However, with few exceptions, these promotions are still controlled by the services because the selection is made by the service chief. The exceptions include the members of the JCS themselves, the directors of the joint service high-level schools, and positions within the Office of the Secretary of Defense. The sanctity of service control over the promotion system was underscored again when Secretary of Defense Schlesinger tried to take personal control over the three- and four-star appointments. Schlesinger's attempts to intervene even at this high level have aroused wide resentment among the services and Congress.[3]

While the service alone is responsible for creating the field from which the chief will be chosen, the responsibility for the actual selection has been quite diffused. During the past twenty-five years no single pattern for choosing a member of the JCS from the field has emerged. On various occasions the Secretary of Defense, the service secretary, or even the outgoing chief has been the dominant influence in the selection process, sometimes prevailing upon the President to select an individual to whom he is opposed. However, there have been other occasions where the chief executive himself has played the dominant role in choosing the new chief. A great deal depends upon the relationship between the President and the secretaries, the role perceptions of the individuals involved, and the prevailing domestic and international political climate. As Jerry Friedheim, former Assistant Secretary of Defense for Public Affairs, so aptly put it, "Circumstances pick Chiefs of Staff."[4]

Because circumstances do pick Chiefs of Staff, it is sheer folly to speculate that certain individuals are predestined to become members of the JCS. Currently, many Army officers and political commentators are speculating that newly selected Colonel Peter Dawkins (West Point, 1959) is a shoo-in for Chief of Staff. Earl Blaik, Dawkins's football coach at West Point, is alleged to have remarked as far back as 1959, "someday if he stays in the Army, Dawkins will be Chief of Staff." However, even if the Army should promote Dawkins to full general some ten years from now, the Secretary of the Army, the Secretary of Defense, or the President may still decide that another four-star general is more to their liking for the post of Chief of Staff or that Dawkins is too valuable in another command, for example, NATO, to move him to Washington. This was the case with General Andrew Goodpaster, who, like Dawkins, is a Princeton Ph.D. Although Goodpaster is a close friend of President Richard Nixon, he was not appointed as Chief of Staff during Nixon's tenure because the President felt he was irreplaceable at NATO. From his days at West Point, First Captain William Westmoreland, many people felt, was an inevitable choice to be Chief of Staff. But not many people placed his classmate Creighton Abrams in the same category. How many people heard of George Decker or Frederick Weyand before unexpected vacancies thrust them onto the JCS?

The Secretary of Defense has been personally responsible for elevating several men to the JCS. Secretary Charles Wilson prevailed upon Eisenhower to select Admiral Radford as chairman of the Joint Chiefs after Radford had been recommended to Wilson by Senator Taft (R-Ohio). After allowing other people to make the initial selections to his JCS, Robert McNamara fired three of them and replaced them with officers with whom he felt he could work. Melvin Laird selected the dynamic young Admiral Zumwalt over thirty-seven other admirals to be Chief of Naval Operations in order to attempt to alter the traditional behavior patterns of the entrenched naval bureaucracy. Zumwalt was recommended to Laird by former Navy Secretary and Laird confidant Paul Nitze. Laird also insisted that President Nixon name General Abrams to the JCS, in spite of his age and poor health, because of the general's fine performance in Vietnam and his support for the administration's Vietnamization program.

On a few occasions a service secretary's voice has been dominant in the selection process. Navy Secretaries Charles Thomas and John Connally insisted that Arleigh Burke and George Anderson be their respective CNOs. Thomas was a personal friend of Burke's, while Connally interviewed approximately a hundred admirals before choosing Anderson.

Sometimes the outgoing chief is asked to recommend a successor and on some occasions he has had the opportunity to select his own relief. The first five Air Force Chiefs of Staff essentially handpicked their own successors by making their nominees the vice-chief of staff at least a year before the end of their own terms. In this way, Generals Vandenberg, Twining, White, Lemay, and McConnell were succeeded by men whose careers and outlooks closely paralleled their own. Chief of Naval Operations David McDonald consciously groomed his fellow naval aviator, Thomas Moorer, to succeed him by placing Moorer in command of both the Atlantic and Pacific fleets. Maxwell Taylor had President Kennedy select his protegé, Earl Wheeler, to serve as Army Chief of Staff, and Wheeler was responsible for his operations deputy, Harold Johnson, moving up to take his place when he succeeded Taylor as chairman.

While the Secretary of Defense, the service secretary, or the outgoing chief may have been the primary mover in the selection of a chief, the President is usually not opposed to their choice. However, on at least two occasions subordinates have convinced the President to nominate to the JCS a man to whom the chief executive was personally opposed. President Eisenhower was initially cool to the appointment of Admirals Radford and Burke because of their role in the "revolt of the admirals," but gave in to the strong pleadings of Secretaries Wilson and Thomas.

Finally, there have been instances when the President himself has been directly involved in the selection process. President Eisenhower personally chose as his Army Chiefs of Staff three men who had worked closely with him in World War II. Moreover, Eisenhower's first choice as Chief of Naval Operations was Robert Carney, who had worked with him during his own days at SHAPE (Supreme Headquarters, Allied Powers, Europe). John Kennedy brought Maxwell Taylor out of retirement to serve as his chairman because of the respect that he had gained for Taylor during his days in the Senate and from Taylor's book *The Uncertain Trumpet*. Finally, Lyndon Johnson selected William Westmoreland as Army Chief of Staff because of the loyal and sometimes public support that Westmoreland had given Johnson's controversial Vietnam policies and because of the rapport that he and his fellow southerner Westmoreland had developed while the latter was serving as the Vietnam commander.

Thus far, we have been discussing the JCS as a group or at the aggregate level. However, one should never lose sight of the fact that an officer comes to the Joint Chiefs only by first rising to the top of his service. Therefore, let us now turn to a consideration of the individual careers of those men who have risen to the top of their services and of the field from which chiefs are selected.

ARMY: THE INDIVIDUALS

When the National Security Act was passed in late 1947, General of the Army Dwight Eisenhower was serving as Army Chief of Staff. However, "Ike" had already expressed a desire to retire from the Army to become president of Columbia University, and on December 1, 1947, Omar Bradley, his West Point classmate, was named to succeed him. Quiet and bespectacled, with a professorial look and manner, Bradley was an infantry officer who graduated from West Point forty-forth in the class of 1915, well ahead of Eisenhower. He did not see action in World War I and spent the inter-war years either as an instructor or as a student at various army schools, primarily at West Point and the infantry school. His only significant nonschool assignment was as assistant secretary to the General Staff. However, because of his association with General Marshall at the infantry school and in Washington, he became the first member of his class to be selected for flag rank.

After World War II broke out, Bradley was placed in charge of the 86th Infantry in Louisiana and then moved to the 28th Division in Florida. He went to the European theater in early 1943 and remained there until the German surrender. Although he did not achieve the notoriety of Eisenhower or the fame of Patton, he was an effective and brilliant field commander, admired by his men and highly respected by his contemporaries. Bradley commanded the II Corps in Northern Africa and Sicily, the 1st Army in the Normandy invasion, and the 12th Army Group in the drive across Europe. The latter assignment was the largest field command in American history. It consisted of four armies and 1.3 million American soldiers. After the war, Bradley became head of the Veterans' Administration. He was serving in that position when he was tapped to succeed Eisenhower. Bradley held the Army's top position for eighteen months when a 1949 amendment to the National Security Act created the position of Chairman of the JCS.

When Bradley was named to be the first chairman of the JCS, his vice-chief of staff, "Lightning Joe" Collins, was selected to succeed him as Army Chief of Staff. One of the few Catholics to head the Army, Collins was an infantry officer and a 1917 graduate of West Point. He spent World War I on various posts in the United States, and the greatest part of the inter-war years as a student or an instructor. During World War II he was one of the few high ranking Army officers to see action in both the Pacific and European theaters and became one of the most daring and aggressive field commanders in American history. He commanded the 25th Infantry Division in the battles of Guadalcanal and New Georgia. During those engagements, his battlefield exploits earned him a Silver Star and the nickname "Lightning Joe." In December 1943, Eisenhower and Bradley requested that he be transferred to Europe to participate in the Normandy invasion. Collins led the VII Corps ashore on D-Day and then across Europe to the Elbe. During the drive, he earned a second Silver Star for his daring breakthrough at St. Lô, called by General Marshall one of the greatest feats of American arms. After the war, Collins was assigned to the Pentagon, where he served as the last director of information for the War Department and First Vice-Chief of Staff in the new Department of the Army.

Collins served as Chief of Staff until his second two-year term was completed, six months after the Eisenhower administration took office. He was succeeded by Matthew Ridgway, one of his West Point classmates. Like Collins, Ridgway was an infantry officer who missed seeing action in World War I. During the interwar years, Ridgway spent about half of his time as a student, attending both Command and General Staff College and the Army War College, or as an instructor, spending six years at West Point. However, he also had a number of politico-military assignments that took him to such places as China, Nicaragua, the Philippines, Panama, and Bolivia.

When World War II broke out, Ridgway was named as Bradley's assistant with the 82nd Infantry Division and, when Bradley was sent to North Africa, he became its commanding general. Shortly thereafter the 82nd Infantry Division was transformed into the first two airborne divisions in Army history, the 82nd and 101st Airborne divisions. Ridgway was given command of the 82nd and shipped overseas with it to North Africa in April

1943. His division took part in the Sicilian campaign and the Normandy invasion, in the latter as part of Collins' VII Corps. In August 1944, Ridgway was moved up to command of the 18th Airborne Corps, which he led in the drive across Europe to the Baltic.

Between WW II and Korea, Ridgway saw duty as a commander in the Mediterranean and Caribbean, and in a politico-military capacity at the United Nations and on the Inter-American Defense Board. When the Korean War broke out, he was serving in the Pentagon as deputy chief of staff for administration. However, within the next two years a series of unexpected events thrust him into some of the Army's most prestigious assignments and ultimately to Chief of Staff. In December 1950 General Walker was killed in a jeep accident in Korea and Ridgway was named to succeed him as commander of the 8th Army. Four months later MacArthur was fired and Ridgway succeeded him as the Supreme Commander in the Far East. Two years later Eisenhower resigned from SHAPE to run for President and Ridgway was selected to take his place. After two years in Europe, Ridgway came back to Washington as Chief of Staff.

Ridgway's time as Army Chief of Staff proved to be the most frustrating of his thirty-eight-year Army career. He disagreed with Eisenhower's concept of professionalism and the President's ideas on military strategy. Thus, when the end of his first two years in office coincided with his sixtieth birthday, Ridgway asked to retire. His request was happily accepted by Eisenhower. However, he was succeeded by Maxwell Taylor, a man whose career and ideas on military strategy closely paralleled his own.

Maxwell Taylor, the soldier-scholar, graduated fourth in the West Point class of 1922. He was originally commissioned into the Corps of Engineers, but four years after his graduation he switched into the field artillery. Prior to World War II, Taylor spent much of his time becoming proficient in foreign languages. He also attended the Command and General Staff School and the

Army War College and taught for four years at West Point. When World War II broke out, he was serving in the office of the secretary of the General Staff. However, when Ridgway, his former Spanish instructor at West Point and his classmate at Command and General Staff, requested him as chief of staff of the 82nd, he left Washington. Taylor went overseas as an artillery commander with the 82nd Airborne and fought in the Sicilian and Italian campaigns. Just prior to D-Day he became commander of the Army's other airborne division, the 101st, and parachuted with it into Normandy and then led it across central Europe. Prior to the invasion of Italy, Taylor volunteered to participate in one of the most dangerous missions of the war. He went behind enemy lines to confer with leading Italian figures about the feasibility of an airborne assault on Rome.

After the war, Taylor became the second youngest superintendent of West Point and the first U.S. commander in Berlin. He served most of the Korean War as deputy chief of staff for operations and administration, but six months before the armistice Collins placed him in command of the 8th Army. After the end of hostilities, Taylor remained in the Far East and in April 1955 he took over the entire Far East Command. He had only served in that post three months when Ridgway's sudden retirement left the post of Chief of Staff vacant.

Although he too found his years as Army Chief of Staff frustrating, Taylor served a full four-year term before retiring. He was succeeded in July 1959 by Lyman Lemnitzer, who was one month short of his sixtieth birthday. He had graduated from West Point two years before Taylor and had succeeded him in the Far East Command. Lemnitzer was an artillery officer who spent the time between the wars alternating between troop duty and service as a student and instructor at various Army schools, including four years at West Point. During this period Lemnitzer acquired a reputation as a brilliant marksman and military planner. Lemnitzer spent most of World War II on the staffs of Eisenhower and Field

Marshal Harold Alexander. He became renowned for participation in two secret missions. In 1943, he was smuggled into North Africa to inform French officials of the invasion, and in 1945 he entered Switzerland in civilian clothes to arrange for the surrender of German troops in Italy and southern Austria.

Between World War II and Korea, Lemnitzer served in a number of staff positions in Washington and Europe. During the Korean War, he commanded the 7th Infantry Division in some of the war's bloodiest battles, and at the age of fifty-three was awarded the Silver Star for conspicuous gallantry. From 1952 to 1955, Lemnitzer served as deputy chief of staff for plans and research. When Taylor moved up to the Far East Command in April 1955, Lemnitzer succeeded him as commander of the 8th Army, and when Taylor was promoted to Chief of Staff, Lemnitzer took his place as Far East commander. In 1957, Taylor chose Lemnitzer to be his vice-chief of staff and at the end of Taylor's tour, thirty-nine years after leaving West Point, he was selected by Eisenhower for the Army's top position.

Lemnitzer was in the Chief of Staff position for about one year when the sudden illness of Air Force General Nate Twining left the position of chairman vacant. Since Eisenhower believed in rotating the chairmanship, he moved Lemnitzer up and made George Decker, the vice-chief, the new Army Chief of Staff. Decker, a specialist in logistics and military economics, and with a reputation in Army circles as a brilliant fiscal expert, was commissioned into the infantry after his graduation from Lafayette College in 1924 with a degree in economics.

Prior to World War II, Decker spent most of his time on troop assignments in the United States. During the war, he served in the Pacific as chief of staff with the 6th Army. He participated in the New Guinea campaign and the invasion of the Philippines, acquiring a reputation for coolness under fire. General Walter Krueger, commander of the 6th Army, said of him: "You could set a bomb off under his desk and he wouldn't turn a hair."

After the war, Decker was assigned to the Army's service force, and served as commander of the 5th Infantry Division. He was not involved in the Korean War. Instead, from 1950 through 1955, he worked in the Pentagon, first as chief of the budget division and later as comptroller of the Army. During the next two years, Decker served in Europe, first as commander of the VII Corps and later as deputy commander of the European Command. In July 1957 he relieved Lemnitzer as the Far East commander, in August 1959 he relieved him as vice-chief, and in September 1960 as Army Chief of Staff. Decker was the first non–West Pointer to become chief since George Marshall, and the first chief in two decades not to have been a protegé of Marshall.

Decker served only two years as Chief of Staff and in the fall of 1962 was succeeded by Earl Wheeler. Decker's lack of dynamism, the fact that he was an Eisenhower holdover, and his involvement with the Bay of Pigs kept him from receiving the normal two-year extension. His successor graduated from West Point with the class of 1932 and was commissioned in the infantry. Prior to the outbreak of World War II, except for a year at infantry school and another at West Point, Wheeler spent all of his service in the field. He spent most of World War II in this country in school and in training assignments. Four months before the German surrender, Wheeler was sent overseas as chief of staff of the 63rd Infantry Division.

Except for one year as commanding officer of the 351st Infantry Brigade, Wheeler spent the time between 1945 and 1958 in the Pentagon or on headquarters staffs. In 1958, he was given command of the 2nd Armored Division at Fort Hood and in 1959 he added the additional duties of III Corps commander. From 1960 to 1962, he served as director of the Joint Staff. One of his duties in this position was to brief candidate John Kennedy on world developments. In March 1962, Wheeler was appointed as Lauris Norstad's deputy in NATO with the expectation that he would succeed Norstad when the latter retired in November 1962. However, in order to remove Lemnitzer as chairman of the JCS "grace-fully," Lemnitzer was given the NATO command and Wheeler was brought back to Washington as Chief of Staff.

When Maxwell Taylor left the Pentagon to go to Saigon as American ambassador, General Wheeler moved up to the chairmanship and his operations deputy, Harold Johnson, succeeded him as Chief of Staff. For Johnson this was a fitting reward and tribute to his determination and courage in the face of adversity. Johnson graduated from West Point one year after Wheeler and was commissioned into the infantry. Prior to the war, Johnson served with various infantry regiments. When the Japanese attacked Pearl Harbor, Johnson was serving with the 57th Infantry in the Philippines. When the islands fell to the Japanese, he was captured and participated in the infamous "Bataan death march." The Japanese imprisoned him in the Philippines until late 1944, when he was moved to Japan and then to Korea. His time as a POW took a terrible toll, and by the end of the war Johnson had lost 80 of his 170 pounds. The American doctor who examined him at the time of his repatriation proclaimed that there was no medical reason why Harold Johnson should have been alive. As a result of this experience, Johnson gained an intense religious faith and zeal that after manifested itself publicly. One of his subordinates remarked that whatever unit Johnson was assigned to had no need of a chaplain. As Chief of Staff, Johnson proscribed foul language by training instructors.

Johnson's internment not only set him back physically but cut him off from the accelerated developments in military tactics that occurred in World War II. In an effort to catch up to his contemporaries, Johnson studied at both the Command and General Staff and the Armed Forces Staff colleges between World War II and Korea. The outbreak of the Korean War provided him with the opportunity to reenter the Army's mainstream. Johnson was one of the first Americans into action. He took the 1st Provisional Infantry Battalion into Korea in August 1950 and remained in that beleaguered country for fifteen months. He was involved in the defense of Pusan, the pursuit to the Yalu, the Chinese invasion, and the subsequent withdrawal below the 38th parallel.

From 1951 through 1960 he alternated between staff duty in Washington and headquarters duty in Europe. He never received command at the division level but was the assistant commander of the 8th Infantry Division for twenty months. In 1960, Johnson became commandant of the Command and General Staff College and in 1963 was selected by Wheeler to be his deputy chief of staff for operations, i.e., General Wheeler's "ops deputy." One year later when Wheeler became chairman, Johnson was selected by McNamara over forty-three other generals to become Wheeler's successor. The defense secretary chose him because of his uncritical acceptance of McNamara's new methods in the Pentagon.

After Johnson had completed his four-year term, William Westmoreland, the Vietnam commander, was named to succeed him. Westmoreland's "promotion" signified a change in our Vietnam strategy but was also a reward for his loyal support for Lyndon Johnson's war strategy. The "inevitable" general and *Time* magazine's Man of the Year in 1965, Westmoreland graduated from West Point in 1936 and was commissioned in the field artillery. Although he ranked 112th in a class of 276, he was the first captain of cadets, the regimental commander, recipient of the Pershing Award for military proficiency and leadership, and marked even then as a potential Chief of Staff by his classmates. Prior to World War II, Westmoreland served with artillery units in Oklahoma and Hawaii. In April 1942, he was sent to North Africa as a battalion commander. He commanded the 34th Field Artillery battalion in combat in Tunisia and Sicily, where his unit won the presidential unit citation. During the Normandy invasion and the drive across Europe, Westmoreland was attached to the 9th Infantry Division. His surehanded manner of command impressed his superiors, including Maxwell Taylor, who recorded his name in a "little black book" that he used to make notes of exceptional officers.

Between World War II and Korea, Westmoreland served with the staffs of the 71st Infantry and the 82nd Airborne divisions and as an instructor in the Command and General Staff and the Army War colleges. He saw action in Korea as commander of an airborne regimental team. From 1953 through 1958, Westmoreland served in the Pentagon on the Army staff in various capacities, including secretary of the general staff under Maxwell Taylor. During those five years in the Pentagon, Westmoreland took time out to spend three months as a student in the advanced management program at the Harvard Business School.

In 1958, Westmoreland, the youngest major general in the Army, was given command of Taylor's old unit, the 101st Airborne. Two years later he became the third youngest superintendent of the military academy. After serving for three years at West Point, Westmoreland spent six months as commander of the 17th Airborne Corps and in January 1964 was detailed to Vietnam as deputy commander of the Military Assistance Command (MACV). In June 1964, Westmoreland relieved Paul Harkins as commander of MACV and spent the next four years presiding over the expansion of his command from 20,000 men to nearly 600,000. However, when Westmoreland was relieved of his Vietnam command and arrived at his "predestined" position of Chief of Staff, he did not come to that position in the manner he expected. His reputation as a field commander was besmirched by the disastrous battlefield tactics he employed in Vietnam, and his reputation as a good general officer was suspect because of his insensitivity to the race and drug problems in his command. His contemporaries who had labelled him as a future Chief of Staff now saw his elevation to that position as a graceful way of firing him from MACV.

Although he continued to display the same inability to grasp complex problems as he had in Vietnam, Westmoreland was allowed to complete a normal four years as Army Chief of Staff. In 1972 he was succeeded by Creighton Abrams, his former classmate and the man who followed him in Vietnam. Rough and rugged in both manner and appearance, the tenth postwar Army Chief of Staff was a cavalry officer who spent all of World War II in Europe with the 4th Armored Division, rising from regimental adjutant to command of a tank battalion.

Between World War II and Korea, Abrams attended Command and General Staff College and the Army War College, and he saw duty in Europe with the 1st Infantry Division. In Korea, Abrams served as chief of staff for three different corps. Between Korea and Vietnam, he spent seven years on the Army staff and four years in Europe, commanding the Tank Armored Division and the V Corps. His staff positions included vice-chief of staff under Harold Johnson. In 1967 he became Westmoreland's deputy at MACV and in July 1968 he became the commander. Four years later, after achieving remarkable success on the ground in Vietnam and successfully presiding over the American withdrawal from Vietnam, Abrams was named Army Chief of Staff at the insistence of Secretary of Defense Laird. His confirmation was held up for three months because of allegations that he had been a party to the unauthorized bombing of North Vietnam by General Lavelle. He was completely exonerated and served on the JCS until his untimely death on September 4, 1974. His success in Vietnam and as Army Chief of Staff was in marked contrast to his former classmate. When Abrams died, he was hailed by President Ford and Secretary of Defense Schlesinger as a genuine American hero.

ARMY: A COMPOSITE

Army combat officers, from whom the Chief of Staff must be selected, are divided into three branches: armored, artillery, and infantry. The ten postwar Army chiefs, whose background data are listed in table 4, have reflected the strength of their respective branches. Six of the ten Army chiefs have come from the largest branch, the infantry. The artillery branch has produced three chiefs and the smallest branch, the armored, only one.

All of the appointees, with the exception of George Decker, graduated from West Point. Decker, who received his commission from the ROTC unit of Lafayette University in 1924, is one of the eight Army Chiefs of Staff in the Army's long history who have not graduated from the military academy, but he is the first chief in the post–World War II era with that distinction. The nine other chiefs represent seven classes from the academy. The classes of 1917 and 1936 each produced two future leaders. J. Lawton Collins and Matthew Ridgway, the second and third postwar chiefs, were members of the class of 1917, while Creighton Abrams and William Westmoreland, the ninth and tenth chiefs, graduated together in 1936.

Postgraduate education in military schools[5] has been an integral part of a future chief's career pattern. All of the chiefs except Westmoreland are graduates of both the staff and the war colleges, and two chiefs have found time to attend three military postgraduate institutions. Moreover, Westmoreland did attend the advanced management program at Harvard and was on the faculty of the Army's Command and General Staff and War colleges. Westmoreland's rapid promotions during World War II made him too senior to attend either school. Johnson attended both the Armed Forces Staff College and the Army Command and General Staff College because his four years as a POW of the Japanese during World War II had placed him far behind his contemporaries. Collins spent a year at the Army's Industrial College.[6] Six chiefs graduated from the Army War College,[7] while Decker, Johnson, and Wheeler attended the National War College.

The average age of those appointed to the Army's top position is fifty-five years. Harold Johnson at fifty-two is the youngest man to reach the top, while Lyman Lemnitzer at fifty-nine is the

TABLE 4

Background Data on the Army Chiefs of Staff

Name	Branch	Source & Year of Commission	Postgraduate	Age	Years of			Tenure Years & Months	Post-C/S
					Service	Flag	4-Star		
Bradley	Infantry	USMA[a]—1915	CGS[b], AWC[c]	55	33	7	3	1 + 6	Chairman
Collins	Infantry	USMA—1917	CGS, AWC, AIC[d]	53	32	7	2	4 + 0	Military Committee NATO
Ridgway	Infantry	USMA—1917	CGS, AWC	58	36	11	3	2 + 0	Retired
Taylor	Artillery	USMA—1922	CGS, AWC	53	33	13	−1	4 + 0	Chairman
Lemnitzer	Artillery	USMA—1920	CGS, AWC	59	39	17	4	1 + 2	Chairman NATO
Decker	Infantry	ROTC—1924	CGS, National[e]	58	36	16	4	2 + 0	Retired
Wheeler	Infantry	USMA—1932	CGS, National	54	30	10	1	1 + 11	Chairman

TABLE 4 (continued)

Name	Branch	Source & Year of Commission	Postgraduate	Age	Service	Years of Flag	4-Star	Tenure Years & Months	Post-C/S
Johnson	Infantry	USMA—1933	CGS AFSCᶠ National	52	31	8	—	4 + 0	Retired
Westmoreland	Artillery	USMA—1936	Harvard	54	32	16	5	4 + 0	Retired
Abrams	Armor	USMA—1936	CGS AWC	58	36	15	8	2 + 0	Died in office
Composite	Infantry	USMA	CGS AWC	55	34	12	3	2 + 6	Retired

49

oldest appointee. It has taken an average of thirty-four years of service as a commissioned officer to become Chief of Staff. Earl Wheeler, who was selected thirty years after graduation from West Point, rose most rapidly, while Lemnitzer, who toiled for thirty-nine years in the ranks, took the most time. All of the appointees had served at least seven years as a general officer, with an average of twelve years. Bradley had the least time as a flag officer, while Lemnitzer, with seventeen years, served the longest. Eight of the appointees were full four-star generals at the time of their selection. Abrams, who had been a full general for eight years before being selected, had the most time in that grade. Johnson, who had been a lieutenant general for only one year and was junior to forty-two other officers when he was selected to succeed Wheeler in 1964, is the lowest ranking officer to become Army Chief of Staff.

The ten chiefs who have already completed their terms have served an average of two years and six months in office. The first chief, Omar Bradley, served the shortest time, only one year and six months, while three chiefs, Taylor, Johnson, and Westmoreland, have served the normal four-year term. No Army chief has ever had his term extended beyond the statutory limit. There are three reasons why the tours of Army chiefs have been so much shorter than the normal four years. First, one-third of the Army chiefs have had their tours interrupted in order to move up to chairman. Bradley, Lemnitzer, and Wheeler all served rather short times as Army chiefs but spent longer periods as chairman. Wheeler served six years as chairman, Bradley four, and Lemnitzer two. Second, two Army chiefs reached the statutory retirement age after completion of their initial two-year tour and were forcibly retired by administrations whose ideas and styles were not compatible with theirs. Ridgway retired on his sixtieth birthday after only two years as Chief of Staff because his strategic concepts clashed headlong with Eisenhower's massive retaliation strategy. Likewise, the Kennedy administration allowed George

Decker, who was a holdover from the Eisenhower administration, to retire in 1962 to make room for their "favorite general," Maxwell Taylor, and his protegé, Earl Wheeler, on the JCS. Decker was not even consulted about his retirement. He heard about Wheeler's appointment as Army Chief of Staff and Taylor's elevation to chairman of the JCS while he was on an inspection trip to Panama. Third, Creighton Abrams died after only two years in office.

In analyzing the career patterns of the ten Army Chiefs of Staff, it is clear that there are many paths to general officer. However, after selection to flag rank, it appears that there are seven key jobs at the general officer level which are stepping-stones to the Army's top position. As indicated in table 5, four of these jobs can be classified as operational, while another three may be considered staff. The operational jobs are commands at the division, corps, army, and joint or unified levels. Nine of the ten chiefs have commanded at least one division. Two men, Bradley and Lemnitzer, have been in charge of two divisions, but only Lemnitzer has had two different kinds of divisions, the 11th Airborne and the 7th Infantry. Harold Johnson never had his own division but was the assistant commander of the 8th Infantry Division from 1956 to 1957. Infantry and airborne divisions appear to be slightly better as jumping-off points. Three of the future chiefs have commanded infantry and another three airborne divisions, while Lemnitzer had one of each. Only Wheeler and Abrams commanded armored divisions.

Seven have had command at the corps level. Maxwell Taylor and Lyman Lemnitzer skipped this level of command on their way to command of a complete army, and Harold Johnson never reached command at the division level. These seven men commanded five different corps, both Ridgway and Westmoreland commanded the XVIII Corps, while Decker and Collins are alumni of the VII Corps. Seven chiefs have also commanded an entire army. Bradley commanded the 1st Army in Europe during World

TABLE 5

Career Patterns of Army Chiefs of Staff: Command and Staff

Name	Division	COMMAND Corps	COMMAND Army	COMMAND Unified	Deputy	STAFF Vice	Other
Bradley	82 INF / 28 INF	2	1	12 Group	—	—	VA
Collins	25 INF	7	—	—	Plans	1	Director of Information
Ridgway	82 AB	18	8	Med / FE / Europe	OPS & ADW	—	UN
Taylor	101 AB	—	8	FE	OPS & ADM	—	USMA
Lemnitzer	11 AB	—	8	FE	Plans & Research	2	NWC
Decker	7 INF / 5 INF	7	8	FE	Comptroller	1	—
Wheeler	2 ARM	3	—	—	—	—	Director of Joint Staff
Johnson	—	—	—	—	Operations	—	CGS
Westmoreland	101 AB	18	VNM	MACV	—	—	USMA
Abrams	3 ARM	5	VNM	MACV	Reserve	3	—

War II, Ridgway and Taylor handled the 8th Army during the Korean War, while Lemnitzer and Decker were in charge of the 8th in the immediate post-armistice period. Westmoreland and Abrams were the commanding generals of the U.S. Army during the war in Vietnam. Neither Collins nor Wheeler held command beyond the corps level.

The seven men who commanded at the army level also moved beyond this level to what may be called a joint or unified or area command. General Bradley commanded the 12th Army Group, which comprised four armies, in the latter stages of the war in Europe. Ridgway, Taylor, Lemnitzer, and Decker all moved up from the 8th Army to head the Far East Command. Both Westmoreland and Abrams headed the Military Assistance Command in Vietnam at the same time that they headed the U.S. Army in Vietnam. As MACV, they had operational control over all of the in-country forces in Vietnam. Ridgway had the most experience in the area or joint command level. Immediately after World War II, he headed the Mediterranean Command. In 1951 when Douglas MacArthur was fired, Ridgway succeeded him as commander in the Far East, and in 1952 when Dwight Eisenhower resigned to run for the Presidency, Ridgway took control of the European Command.

It seems clear that when the position of Army Chief of Staff becomes vacant, the place to be is the area command where a shooting war is in progress. Six of the last eight chiefs have come almost directly from the Korean and Vietnam commands. The other two, Wheeler and Johnson, who were appointed during the lull between Korea and Vietnam, were serving in staff positions in Washington. The prestigious European (or NATO) Command does not appear to be a good route to the Army's top job. Ridgway is the only chief to have held this command, and then only briefly, and Lyman Lemnitzer took over the European Command after having served as Army Chief of Staff and chairman of the JCS.

Two positions on the Army staff appear to be stepping stones to Chief of Staff. They are the posts of deputy chief of staff and vice-chief. Seven chiefs have held a position at the deputy level and four of these men have moved up to vice-chief. Only Bradley, Wheeler, and Westmoreland did not see service at the deputy level before taking the Army's top position. Both Bradley and Westmoreland spent the majority of their time as general officers in operational assignments, while Wheeler's nonoperational assignments were in the joint arena. Collins, Lemnitzer, and Decker all held the number two position immediately prior to moving up to the Army's top position. Abrams had a tour in Vietnam between his service as vice-chief and as Chief of Staff.

In addition to service on the Army staff, the great majority of the future chiefs have held a nonoperational position of high visibility. Four of the chiefs headed military schools. Taylor and Westmoreland were superintendents of the U.S. Military Academy, while Johnson and Lemnitzer were commandants of the Command and General Staff College and the National War College, respectively. Bradley was the first postwar director of the Veterans' Administration, and Ridgway was the first U.S. representative on the Military Staff Committee of the United Nations. Collins served as the last director of information for the War Department and Wheeler was the director of the Joint Staff from 1960 to 1962.

NAVY: THE INDIVIDUALS

When the National Security Act was passed, the Navy, like the Army, was headed by one of its five-star officers, Fleet Admiral Chester Nimitz. Like Eisenhower, Nimitz had also indicated a desire to retire, and soon after the creation of the Department of Defense, Nimitz was succeeded as the eleventh Chief of Naval Operations by Louis Denfeld, the Commander in Chief of the Pacific. A 1912 graduate of the Naval Academy, Denfeld served with a destroyer force operating out of Queenstown Island during World War I. Between the wars, Denfeld spent about two-thirds of his time at sea and one-third in shore assignments. His sea duty was mainly in destroyers. Denfeld commanded two destroyers, two destroyer divisions, and one destroyer squadron. He also spent two years on submarine duty and served as commanding officer of the USS *S-24* from August 1923 to June 1924. Denfeld's shore assignments were primarily in Washington, serving with the Bureau of Navigation and as aide to the CNO, Fleet Admiral William Leahy.

During the first part of World War II, Denfeld was entrusted with the organization and development of a task force to convoy shipping from the United States to the United Kingdom. For the greatest part of the war, Denfeld served as assistant chief of naval personnel and managed the rapid expansion of the naval service. During the last six months of the war in the Pacific, he was in charge of Battleship Division 9 and participated in the Okinawan invasion.

After the war ended, Denfeld served for a year as chief of naval personnel, and then moved to the post of Commander in Chief of the Pacific, with collateral duties as Commander in Chief of the Pacific Fleet (CINCPACFLT) and first High Commissioner of the Trust Territories. When he was promoted to Chief of Naval Operations on December 15, 1947, the *New York Times* commented that he possessed one of the Navy's most inquiring minds, a keen understanding of the difficulties of unification of the armed forces, a knowledge of the Navy's air problems, and an appreciation of the public's interest in the naval establishment and of the public's right to full information.

These qualities of Denfeld, enumerated by the *New York Times,* proved his undoing as CNO. He attempted to mediate between the Secretary of Defense and his own service in the unification battle and lost the confidence of both. When he finally sided with his own service during the B-36 controversy by telling the

House Armed Services Committee that administration policies were seriously weakening the Navy in favor of the Air Force and Army, President Truman offered him a post in the Atlantic or dismissal. He chose the latter and was succeeded by Forrest Sherman, the youngest CNO in history and the first aviator to occupy the position.

Sherman graduated with distinction from Annapolis in 1917. He ranked second in a class of 203 and was a regimental adjutant. During World War I he served in the Mediterranean on board a cruiser. Immediately after the war, Sherman commanded a destroyer and then went into flight training. He was designated as a naval aviator in 1922. For the next twenty years Sherman spent most of his time on aircraft carriers, either as a squadron commander or as part of ship's company. He served on board the *Lexington,* the *Saratoga,* and the *Ranger,* and commanded Scouting Squadron 2 and Fighter Squadron 1. His shore assignments included the staff course at the Naval War College, instructor duty at Annapolis, and staff duty at CINCPACFLT.

From 1940 to early 1942, Sherman served in the war plans division in the office of the Chief of Naval Operations and attended the Atlantic Conference as the naval aviation advisor. In May 1942, he assumed command of the carrier *Wasp.* When it was sunk in September 1942, Sherman was awarded the Navy Cross and sent to staff duty with Nimitz, serving as deputy chief of staff for CINCPACFLT. He was the Navy representative at the initial peace conferences with the Japanese at Manila and was present at the formal surrender aboard the USS *Missouri.*

After the War, Sherman commanded Carrier Division 1 briefly and the 6th Fleet for about fifteen months. He also served as deputy CNO for operations from December 1945 through January 1948. While serving in this position, Sherman, working with Lauris Norstad and Clark Clifford, helped draft the National Security Act of 1947, which preserved the independence of the services in the new Department of Defense. It was Clifford who recommended Sherman to Truman after the latter had fired Denfeld.

In July 1951, after only twenty months in office, Sherman suffered a heart attack and died while on an inspection trip to Italy. Of the four full admirals then on active duty in the Navy, only one, William Fechteler, had not been involved in the "revolt of the admirals," and on August 1, 1951, Fechteler was named to succeed Sherman. William Fechteler was the second son of Rear Admiral August Fechteler and the younger brother of Lieutenant Frank Fechteler, who was killed in World War I and for whom a heavy destroyer was christened in 1945. Fechteler graduated from Annapolis in 1916, ranked eighteenth in a class of 177. During World War I, he served on board the battleship *Pennsylvania,* the flagship of the Atlantic fleet, in European waters as aide to the fleet commander. Between world wars, Fechteler commanded the destroyer *Perry,* was a battleship gunnery officer, and held various destroyer staff billets. He also had shore duty at the Naval Academy and in Washington.

For the first eighteen months of World War II, Fechteler served as assistant director of the Bureau of Naval Personnel. In August 1943, he took command of the battleship *Indiana* and in January 1944 became commander of Amphibious Group 8. In this capacity Fechteler directed ten amphibious operations in New Guinea and the Philippines. Between 1945 and 1950, Fechteler served as assistant chief of naval personnel under Denfeld, deputy CNO for personnel under Sherman, and as commander of battleships and cruisers of the Atlantic Fleet. On February 1, 1950, he was named as the Commander in Chief of the Atlantic Fleet (CINCLANTFLT) by Sherman and was serving in that capacity when he was nominated for CNO.

In order to sweep Fechteler out of office with the entire JCS in the summer of 1953, Eisenhower named Fechteler commander in chief of the Allied Forces in Southern Europe and replaced him as CNO with Robert Carney, his Naval Academy classmate.

Carney also graduated with distinction from Annapolis in 1916. He saw action as a gunnery and torpedo officer on destroyers in World War I. Between the wars, he commanded two destroyers and a cargo ship and served as a gunnery officer on the cruiser *Cincinnati* and as executive officer of the battleship *California*. Carney also served on several fleet staffs, as an instructor at the Naval Academy, and in the Secretary of the Navy's office.

In the initial stages of World War II, Carney was assigned to the staff of the Atlantic Fleet's support force. There he developed plans for protecting shipping against submarines. In October 1942, Carny was sent to the Pacific and remained there until the Japanese surrender. From October 1942 till August 1943, he commanded the cruiser *Denver* in the Solomons campaign and sank two Japanese destroyers. For the remainder of the war, he served as chief of staff to Admiral Halsey. In this position he formulated the plans for the numerous combat operations in which Halsey's 3rd Fleet participated and he received the Navy Cross for extraordinary heroism in the Battle of Leyte Gulf.

After the war, Carney served as deputy CNO for logistics under Nimitz, Denfeld, and Sherman. In March 1950, he took command of the 2nd Fleet and six months later became commander in chief of naval forces in the eastern Atlantic and the Mediterranean. In June 1951, General Eisenhower selected Carney to be his deputy at NATO and gave him the additional title of commander in chief of the Allied Forces in Southern Europe. Two years later President Eisenhower picked Admiral Carney as the fourth postwar CNO.

Carney reached his sixtieth birthday after eighteen months in office, and upon completion of his first two-year term he retired and was succeeded by Arleigh Burke. Although he was one of the best known and most colorful Navy officers, the selection of "31 Knot Burke" surprised many people. At the time of his selection he was ranked below ninety-two other admirals and was the first two-star officer ever promoted to the JCS. He was so "junior" that when he became CNO he was only promoted to vice admiral.

Burke graduated from Annapolis in 1923. His classmates at the Naval Academy recall that he was an exceptionally serious student interested only in learning to be a naval officer. At the academy he had no time either for athletics or for midshipmen's monkey business. Prior to World War II, Burke served on battleships and destroyers and commanded one destroyer. His shore duty consisted of assignments at the Bureau of Ordnance and two years of postgraduate work in engineering. In June 1931, he received an M.S. in engineering from the University of Michigan.

For the first year of World War II, much to his chagrin, Burke was with the inspection division of the naval gun factory in Washington. He was sent overseas to the South Pacific in January 1943 and for the next year commanded destroyer divisions and squadrons. From October 1943 to March 1944 he led Destroyer Squadron 23, the "Little Beavers," to spectacular victories in the Solomons. The "Little Beavers" fought in 22 separate engagements and sank one cruiser, nine destroyers, one submarine, several smaller ships, and thirty aircraft, and earned a presidential unit citation. Because he once radioed to some transports in his path, "Stand aside. I'm coming through at 31 knots," he acquired his nickname from Admiral Halsey. For the remainder of the war, Burke served as chief of staff to the commander of Fast Carrier Task Force 58. During the Okinawan campaign Burke was on board two aircraft carriers sunk by kamikaze aircraft. For rescuing several people from these ships and for maintaining control of the task force during the attacks, Burke was awarded a silver star.

Between 1945 and 1948, Burke served with the Bureau of Ordnance again and on staff duty in the Atlantic. In January 1948 he became the assistant to CNO Denfeld in the organizational research and policy division, known as OP-23. As head of this office, Burke was in charge of preparing the Navy's presentation for the House Armed Services Committee investigation into the cancellation of the supercarrier. Because of the activities of this office, Burke's name was removed from the promotion list by the Secretary of the Navy, but under pressure from House Republicans, Truman restored Burke's name and he became an admiral in July 1950.

After the outbreak of the Korean War, Burke became deputy chief of staff to the commander of the naval forces in the Far East and then took command of Cruiser Division 5 in Korean waters. From July 1951 to early 1952 he served as a member of the United Nations' truce delegation at Panmunjon. For the next two and a half years Burke was assigned to the office of the CNO as director of the Strategic Plans Division under Fechteler and Carney. In April 1954 he took command of Cruiser Division 6, and in January 1955 he assumed command of the Atlantic Fleet's destroyer force. Six months later Carney retired and Burke became CNO.

Burke served six stormy years as Chief of Naval Operations and in 1961 turned down President Kennedy's offer of a fourth two-year term. He was succeeded by George Anderson, a Brooklyn-born admiral who was selected by Secretary of the Navy John Connally after the latter had interviewed 109 admirals, about 10 of whom were senior to the selectee. Anderson graduated twenty-seventh in the Naval Academy's class of 1927. After a short tour on board a battleship, Anderson entered flight training and became a naval aviator in 1930. Prior to World War II, he served with fighter and patrol squadrons and on board the carrier *Yorktown*. During the early days of World War II, he was with the Plans Division of the Bureau of Aeronautics formulating the American aircraft program for the war. In March 1943 he became the navigator of the carrier *Yorktown* and was aboard this ship for its first six months of action in the Pacific. For the remainder of the war Anderson served on Fleet staffs.

From 1945 to 1948, Anderson was assigned to Navy headquarters, serving as the Navy representative on various joint bodies. During the next five years, he commanded two aircraft carriers, attended the National War College, and served on Eisenhower's NATO staff. From 1953 to 1955, Anderson was a special assistant to Admiral Radford, the chairman of the JCS. Promoted to rear admiral in 1955, he commanded the Taiwan Patrol Force and then served as chief of staff to CINCPAC. In 1958, he reverted to rear admiral to assume command of Carrier Division 6. One year later he was promoted to commander of the 6th Fleet, and in 1961 became the first and only Catholic to be named as the CNO.

On paper Anderson was one of the most qualified men to become a member of the JCS. In addition to his major Navy commands, Anderson had considerable joint experience. His assignment with the Bureau of Aeronautics in the early stages of World War II involved considerable liaison work with the Army. For his efforts he received an Army commendation medal and the plaudits of General Eisenhower. In the immediate postwar period Anderson worked first with the joint planning staff and on the staff of SHAPE. In the 1950s he was an assistant to the chairman of the JCS and was chief of staff to the unified command in the Pacific.

Despite these apparent qualifications, Anderson had a difficult time with a Secretary of Defense who tried to downgrade military judgment. During his two years as CNO, Anderson clashed repeatedly with McNamara over such items as building a common fighter plane for the Navy and Air Force (the TFX) and the conduct of the blockade in the Cuban missile crisis. In the summer of 1963 Anderson was named ambassador to Portugal and David McDonald was brought home from London to succeed him on the JCS.

David McDonald graduated from Annapolis one year after Anderson and had a career that closely paralleled that of his CNO predecessor. McDonald saw battleship service after graduation and then went into flight training. He became a naval aviator in 1931 and spent the pre–World War II period in fighter and patrol squadrons. McDonald spent most of World War II as a flight training officer but saw one year of action in the Pacific as executive officer of the *Essex*.

From the end of the war until his selection for flag rank in 1955, McDonald served in the Pentagon with the Bureau of Aeronautics, attended the National War College, served on the staff of CINCPACFLT, and commanded two aircraft carriers. As an admiral, McDonald first served as the director of the Air Warfare Division in the office of the CNO, and then on the staff of SHAPE. In 1960 he relieved Anderson as commander of Carrier Division 6 and in 1961 relieved him as commander of the 6th Fleet. In April 1963 he was "jumped" over twenty-eight senior vice admirals and made a four-star admiral. Simultaneously, he was given command of all U.S. naval forces in Europe. However, less than one month later, President Kennedy announced that McDonald would succeed Anderson as CNO.

McDonald became the first CNO in the postwar period to serve a normal four-year term, and in the summer of 1967, Thomas Moorer was named to succeed him. Like other members of the JCS, during that period McDonald experienced the frustrations of working with McNamara and the young men that he brought into the Pentagon from the business and academic communities. However, McDonald was able to groom Moorer to be his successor and did convince President Johnson to appoint him as the eighth postwar CNO.

Like McDonald, Moorer was a southerner, an aviator, and an Annapolis graduate. Moorer graduated with the class of 1933, saw service on two battleships, and became a naval aviator in 1936. Prior to the outbreak of the war, Moorer served with fighter and patrol squadrons. He was with a patrol squadron at Pearl Harbor when the Japanese attacked. His squadron was deployed to the Southwest Pacific and, although Moorer only stayed in that area for six months, he saw considerable action. In February 1942, his patrol plane was shot down and the ship that rescued him was sunk. For his actions in landing his damaged plane and aiding in the rescue of survivors from the damaged ship, Moorer was awarded the Silver Star. In May 1942, Moorer was awarded a Distinguished Flying Cross for delivering supplies to a beleaguered garrison and evacuating wounded men. He returned from the Pacific in the summer of 1942 and spent the remainder of the war in the Atlantic theater.

Between the end of the war and his selection for admiral in 1957, Moorer rotated between sea and shore billets, mostly the latter. His sea duty consisted of carrier assignments and command of a seaplane tender. Moorer's shore billets included work with the Joint Strategic Bombing Survey, study at the Naval War College, and assignment to staff duty. He spent four of his first five years as an admiral in the office of the CNO in various capacities. His only tour away from the Pentagon was a year in the Mediterranean as commander of Carrier Division 6. However, Moorer's next five years were spent at sea in some of the Navy's most prestigious assignments. From 1962 to 1964, he commanded the 7th Fleet, then spent a year as commander of the Pacific Fleet and two years as commander of the Atlantic Fleet. On June 3, 1967, he was nominated to succeed McDonald.

Moorer spent three years as CNO before becoming the second naval officer to serve as chairman of the JCS. When President Nixon nominated Moorer to succeed General Wheeler, he startled the Pentagon community by naming 49-year-old Elmo Zumwalt to succeed Moorer as CNO. Zumwalt graduated with distinction from the Naval Academy in 1942 and served as a junior officer on a destroyer in the Pacific during the war. After the cessation of hostilities, he took command of a captured Japanese gunboat and sailed it to Shanghai, where he assisted in disarming the Japanese. Between World War II and Korea, Zumwalt served on three destroyers and with the NROTC unit at the University of North Carolina. During the Korean War, Zumwalt served as navigator of the battleship *Wisconsin*.

Between the end of the Korean War and his selection for rear admiral in 1965, Zumwalt attended the Naval and National War colleges, commanded two destroyers, and spent seven years in the Pentagon. His Washington assignments included senior aide to Secretary of the Navy Paul Nitze and service in the office of the assistant secretary of defense for international security affairs. After he became the youngest officer ever promoted to rear admiral, Zumwalt assumed command of a cruiser destroyer flotilla. In 1966 he established and directed the Systems Analysis Division of the office of the CNO, and from 1968 to 1970 he was the commander of the naval forces in Vietnam. While serving in Vietnam, Paul Nitze, his former boss as Secretary of the Navy and as assistant secretary of defense for international security affairs, recommended him to Secretary of Defense Melvin Laird as a man who could revitalize the Navy in the post-Vietnam period.

Zumwalt spent four years as CNO trying to reshape the naval bureaucracy. His changes were popular with most of the enlisted men and junior officers but were resisted by the more senior officers. Zumwalt's innovations attracted nationwide attention and made him the best known member of the JCS. However, a number of incidents, including race riots on aircraft carriers, marked his tenure in office and he was succeeded by James Holloway III, a third-generation admiral who promised to bring back some of the Navy's traditions.

NAVY: A COMPOSITE

In many respects, the Navy is not one but three services, and the Navy line officers corps can be broken down into three distinct branches: aviation, surface, and submarine. Of the first nine CNOs appointed since the end of World War II, five have been surface officers and four have been aviators. As yet no submariner has held the Navy's top position. Louis Denfeld spent two years with the submarine branch early in his career, but the majority of his service was in battleships and destroyers. However, in view of the ever-increasing percentage of resources being devoted to the silent service,[8] it should be only a matter of time before a submariner becomes CNO. Certainly there ought to be one before the end of this decade.

Thus far the surface-aviator rotation of the Navy's top spot has been somewhat cyclical. Three surface officers ran the Navy during the 1950s, three aviators served as CNO in the 1960s, and a surface officer was in charge for the first part of this decade. Table 6 lists the nine CNOs in chronological order, with pertinent background data.

The Navy remains the only service to be headed only by graduates of its own service academy. All nine CNOs graduated from the Naval Academy. Two of the chiefs, Fechteler and Carney, were members of the class of 1916. A third member of that class, Arthur Radford, became the first Navy man to serve as chairman of the JCS.

Education at the senior service schools did not play a large part in the careers of the chiefs who ran the Navy through 1961. Only one of the first five postwar leaders graduated from any service school at any level. Forrest Sherman, the second CNO, attended the staff course at the Naval War College. However, all of the last four chiefs have attended a service level war college, and Elmo Zumwalt also attended the staff course at the Naval War College. The senior course at the National War College appears to be becoming an important stepping stone to CNO. Three of the last four chiefs are graduates of it. Thomas Moorer, who attended the Navy's war college, is the only CNO since 1961 not to graduate from National. Arleigh Burke, the only CNO and only member of the JCS to hold an advanced degree from a civilian university, possesses an M.S. in engineering from the University of Michigan.

The average age of the CNO at his appointment is just over

TABLE 6

Background Data on Chiefs of Naval Operations

Name	Branch	Source & Year of Commission	Post-Graduate	Age	Service	Years of Flag	4-Star	Tenure Years & Months	Post-CNO
Denfeld	Surface	USNA[a]—1912	–	55	35	5	2	1 + 11	Fired
Sherman*	Air	USNA—1917	NWC(S)[c]	53	32	6	–	1 + 8	Died
Fechteler	Surface	USNA—1916	–	56	35	7	1	2 + 0	CINC South
Carney	Surface	USNA—1916	–	58	37	10	3	2 + 0	Retired
Burke	Surface	USNA—1923	Michigan	53	32	5	–	6 + 0	Retired
Anderson*	Air	USNA—1927	National[d]	54	34	7	–	2 + 0	Fired
McDonald*	Air	USNA—1928	National	56	35	7	1	4 + 0	Retired
Moorer*	Air	USNA—1933	NWC[b]	55	34	9	3	3 + 0	Chairman
Zumwalt	Surface	USNA—1943	NWC(S) National	49	27	5	–	4 + 0	Retired
Composite	Surface	USNA	National	54	33	7	1	2 + 10	Retired

* Aviator
[a] USNA—United States Naval Academy
[b] NWC—Naval War College
[c] NWC(S)—Naval War College (Staff Course)
[d] National—National War College

fifty-four. Zumwalt, who is one of the two men to reach the JCS some months prior to his fiftieth birthday, is by far the youngest man appointed to the Navy's top position. Carney, who was fifty-eight when Eisenhower moved him up during the 1953 house-cleaning, is the oldest. It has taken an average of thirty-three years of service for an individual to move to the top. As might be expected, Zumwalt's rise was the most rapid and Carney's the slowest. The recently retired CNO was selected only twenty-seven years after his graduation from Annapolis, while Carney waited thirty-seven years for his turn.

All of the appointees served at least five years as a flag officer, with an average tenure of seven years. The time spent as a flag officer for naval officers before moving to the JCS is much less than the other services because the Navy has abolished its one-star or 0–7 grade level. All Navy admirals receive two stars at appointment to flag. Only Carney, who spent ten years as a flag officer, deviates very much from the seven-year norm. Zumwalt is one of three officers who spent only five years as a flag officer before being appointed. His rapid rise to the top came prior to his reaching the rank of rear admiral. Zumwalt's advance from rear admiral to CNO was not exceptionally short for a naval officer.

Being one of the Navy's ten full or four-star admirals is not much of an advantage when it comes time for CNO selection. Four of the nine postwar selectees were not full admirals upon receiving their appointment, and an additional chief had been a full admiral for only one month. Burke was only a rear admiral and junior to ninety-eight other line officers when he was selected. Zumwalt, Anderson, and Sherman were vice or three-star admirals and ranked thirty-eighth, eleventh, and tenth on the seniority list when they were selected. McDonald was promoted to full admiral on April 1, 1963, and selected to be CNO on May 6, 1963. The Kennedy administration had decided in early 1963 that McDonald would succeed Anderson and promoted him to full admiral before nominating him in order to placate naval officers and congress-men who were upset over Anderson's firing. No CNO had been a full admiral for more than three years at the time of selection.

The average tenure in office of the Chief of Naval Operations has been two years and ten months. Admiral Zumwalt, who retired as CNO in the summer of 1974, was only the second CNO to complete a normal four-year tour. David McDonald, who served from 1963 to 1967, was the first. Not one of the first six CNOs completed a normal tour. Five of them served two years or less, and Burke served a full six years and turned down an opportunity to serve an additional two years.

There are several reasons for the relatively short tours of the CNOs. Sherman died after only twenty months in office. Two chiefs were fired for publicly criticizing administration policy: Denfeld opposed the decision of the Truman administration to cancel construction of the supercarrier *United States* and joined his fellow admirals who "revolted" against the civilian leadership; Anderson opposed the decision of Robert McNamara to build a common fighter plane for the Air Force and Navy (the F-111) and resisted the secretary's attempt to manage the naval blockade during the Cuban missile crisis. Carney reached his sixtieth birth-day at about the same time that he completed his first two-year term and asked his friend Eisenhower to allow him to retire. Fechteler was a victim of Eisenhower's promise to Senator Taft to purge the Truman chiefs for supporting the Democratic admin-istration's foreign policy. Although General Bradley was Taft's primary target, the Ohio senator insisted that Eisenhower appoint a complete new team and the President "transferred" Fechteler to southern Europe. Finally, Moorer moved up to be chairman before completion of his tour as CNO.

Burke's long tenure in office is paradoxical. He often publicly criticized the Eisenhower administration's defense policies and Eisenhower accused him of "legalized insubordination."[9] How-ever, Burke was an excellent administrator, had great support in

Congress, and, perhaps most important, was able to keep the tra-
ditionally recalcitrant naval officers corps under control.[10] For
example, when the Eisenhower administration placed the Polaris
submarines under the control of the Strategic Air Command, Burke
was able to prevent unhappy Navy officers from subverting the
decision.

Analysis of the career patterns of the CNOs makes it clear
that the primary requisite for flag selection in the Navy is. deep
draft command at sea. All of the future CNOs commanded at least
one large ship prior to becoming an admiral. The surface officers
commanded battleships or cruisers, while the aviators were in
charge of aircraft carriers. Moreover, after flag selection, the path
to CNO is also in the operational realm. All of the Navy chiefs
have held several seagoing commands as flag officers, while none
of them has served in more than one staff billet. Table 7 outlines
the career patterns for the Navy's top men.

There are three levels of command in the operational realm.
At the first level is command of a division or force of ships. The
second level encompasses command of one of the Navy's four
numbered fleets, while the third level includes command in a particular geographic area. Eight of the chiefs held command of a
division or force of ships. Only Carney did not hold command at
this level. He went directly from command of a ship to Halsey's
staff. The four aviators had command of a carrier division, while
the four surface officers were in charge of a group of smaller ships.
All of the aviators who held the reins of power in the last decade
commanded Carrier Division 6, while Sherman commanded Carrier Division 1. Anderson felt that command of a carrier division
was so important that he reverted from three to two stars to get
one. Four of the CNOs held more than one command at this level.
Denfeld commanded two destroyer forces and one battleship force,
Burke led two cruiser forces and one destroyer force, while Fechteler commanded both an amphibious and a combined battleship-
carrier force. Anderson is the only aviator to hold more than one

TABLE 7
Career Patterns of Chiefs of Naval Operations

| Name | OPERATIONAL: COMMAND OF | | | Office of CNO | STAFF | |
	Division or Force	Single Fleet	Area		Deputy	Bureau
Denfeld	DD[a]11 DD 18 BB[b] 9	—	Pacific	—	—	Personnel
Sherman	CD[c] 1	6	Europe	—	Operations	—
Fechteler	Amphib 7 BB/CL[d] (Atlantic)	—	Atlantic	—	Personnel	—
Carney	—	2	Europe	—	Logistics	—
Burke	DD (Atlantic) CL 5 CL 6	—	—	Strategic Plans	—	—
Anderson	Taiwan Patrol	6	—	—	—	—
McDonald	CD 6	6	Europe	Air Warfare	—	—
Moorer	CD 6	7	Pacific Atlantic	Long Range Planning	—	—
Zumwalt	CL/DD 7	—	Vietnam	Systems Analysis	—	—

[a] DD—Destroyer Force   [b] BB—Battleship Force   [c] CD—Carrier Division   [d] CL—Cruiser Force

command at this level. In addition to Carrier Division 6, the former ambassador to Portugal[11] commanded the Taiwan Patrol Force.

Five of the CNOs commanded one of the Navy's four individual fleets. Each of the aviators had his own fleet, while Carney was the only surface officer to hold command at this level. Command of the Mediterranean-based 6th Fleet appears to be the most important stepping-stone to the top. Sherman, Anderson, and McDonald all ran the 6th Fleet at one time in their careers.

Burke and Anderson are the only chiefs not to have held command on the area level. Burke came to the JCS directly from command of destroyer forces in the Atlantic, while Anderson came directly from the 6th Fleet. The other seven chiefs commanded in different areas of the world. Sherman, McDonald, and Carney were in charge of naval forces in Europe. Denfeld commanded the Pacific Fleet and Fechteler the Atlantic Fleet, while Moorer is the only man to command both the Atlantic and Pacific fleets. Zumwalt came to the Pentagon directly from his post as commander of naval forces in Vietnam. Thus far, no one has moved up to CNO from the prestigious position of CINCPAC.

Staff assignments in Washington do not appear to be vital rungs on the ladder to CNO. All of the chiefs have spent the greatest part of their flag years at sea and all moved to the Navy's top position from an operational billet. None of the officers has spent more than a single tour on the Navy staff and Anderson never served in the Pentagon after being selected for rear admiral.[12]

In recent years, assignment to the office of the Chief of Naval Operations has become the one staff position with some significance. Four of the past five chiefs have headed a division within the CNOs office. Burke directed strategic plans; McDonald, air warfare; Moorer, long-range planning; and Zumwalt, systems analysis. In the immediate postwar era, holding the position of deputy CNO was more important. Burke's three predecessors were all deputies of various branches. Denfeld, the first CNO appointed after passage of the National Security Act, is the only CNO to have headed one of the Navy's powerful bureaus. He headed the Bureau of Naval Personnel immediately after the close of World War II. None of the first nine CNOs served as vice-chief of naval operations.

AIR FORCE: THE INDIVIDUALS

When the Air Force was made a separate service in 1947, Carl Spaatz was serving as commander of the Army Air Forces. After passage of the National Security Act, President Truman selected him to be the first Chief of Staff of the new service. Spaatz graduated from West Point in 1914 and was commissioned in the infantry. However, in 1916 he switched into aviation and went to Europe in World War I, where he became an "ace," shooting down three German Fokker planes. Between the wars, Spaatz attended Command and General Staff College, served at several air bases, commanded a bomber group and bomber wing, and was on the Air Staff for six years. In 1929 his plane *Question Mark* set an endurance record by staying aloft for 150 hours.

After the outbreak of World War II, Spaatz was sent to Europe, where he remained until the German surrender. During the war, he commanded the 8th and 12th Air Forces, the Northwest African Air Force, and the U.S. strategic air forces in Europe. After the defeat of Germany, Spaatz took command of the strategic air forces in the Pacific, where he supervised the atomic bombings of Japan. When the Japanese surrendered, he returned to the Pentagon to take command of the Army Air Forces.

When he was nominated to be Chief of Staff, Spaatz agreed to take the position only on an interim basis. His long overseas service in World War II had exhausted him, and Spaatz was anxious to retire. His wishes were respected and nine months later his 49-year-old deputy, Hoyt Vandenberg, became the second Air

Force Chief of Staff. Vandenberg graduated in the bottom 10 percent of the class of 1922 from West Point and was commissioned directly into the Air Service. Prior to the outbreak of World War II, Vandenberg spent considerable time both as a student and as an instructor. He attended the Air Corps Tactical School, the Command and General Staff College, and the Army War College, and was an instructor in flight school and tactical school. Vandenberg also served as commander of a pursuit (fighter) squadron and in the Plans Division of the office of the Chief of the Air Corps.

During the first part of the war, Vandenberg served as chief of staff to Spaatz, first with the 12th Air Force and then with the Northwest African Strategic Air Force. He returned to the United States in August 1943 as deputy chief of the Air Staff. In early 1944, Vandenberg became head of the air mission to the Soviet Union and in April 1944 was assigned to Eisenhower's staff in London as deputy commander of the Allied Expeditionary Air Forces. Four months later, he assumed command of the 9th Tactical Air Force, which participated in the Normandy invasion and supported the drive of Allied forces across Europe, making 400,000 flights in nineteen months, destroying 4,000 German planes and 6,500 tanks.

In January 1946, Vandenberg became the first director of Central Intelligence. He served in this position until June 1947, when he became Spaatz's deputy, his vice-chief of staff.

Vandenberg's second two-year term expired in the spring of 1952. Because the Korean War was still in progress and because he had decided not to seek reelection, President Truman extended Vandenberg's term for an additional year. Thus, Vandenberg did not step down from the Air Force's top position until June 30, 1953, after five years and two months in the post. He was succeeded by Nathan Twining, who had been his vice-chief of staff since July 1950. Twining graduated from West Point five years before Vandenberg with the class of 1918. He stood in the middle of his class and was commissioned into the infantry. Twining saw brief service in World War I and attended the Infantry School immediately after the war. He entered flight training in 1923 and was transferred to the Air Service in 1926. Prior to World War II, Twining attended Command and General Staff College and the Air Corps Tactical School. He also commanded an attack squadron and served in a variety of technical assignments at various air fields.

Twining saw action in both the Pacific and European theaters and with the tactical and strategic air forces during the War. He served in the Pacific for eighteen months, first as chief of staff to the commander of Army Forces, and then in the dual role of commander of the 13th Air Force and as commander of all U.S. and Allied air forces in the Solomons. Twining was shot down in January 1943 and was adrift for six days in a life raft before being rescued. In November 1943, he took command of the 15th Air Force in Italy and of all the Allied strategic air forces in the Mediterranean. After the surrender in Europe, he returned to the Pacific to assume command of the 20th Air Force. It was a plane from this unit which dropped the atomic bomb on Hiroshima.

After the war, Twining took command of the Air Material Command and then the Alaskan Command. In July 1950, he became deputy chief of staff for personnel and three months later moved up to be the vice-chief of staff.

After four years as Air Force Chief of Staff, Twining became the first Air Force officer to become chairman of the JCS and he was succeeded as Chief of Staff by Thomas White, his own deputy. White is the youngest man ever to graduate from West Point. He was one month short of his nineteenth birthday when he graduated with the class of 1920 and was commissioned into the infantry. After attending infantry school and serving with an infantry division, White entered flight training. In 1925 he became a member of the Air Service, but did not spend much time in aviation billets. Over the next fifteen years he studied Chinese in Peking and served as an attaché in the Soviet Union, Italy, Greece, and Brazil. His other assignments included Command and General Staff College, language studies at Georgetown University, and staff duty on the Air Staff.

White spent the first three years of World War II in the United States as chief of staff for the 3rd Air Force in Tampa, Florida, and as assistant chief of the Air Staff for intelligence. He was assigned to the Southwest Pacific in September 1944 as deputy commander of the 13th Air Force and in June 1945 took command of the 7th Air Force during the Okinawan campaign.

After the war, White became chief of staff of the Pacific Air Command and then took over the 5th Air Force. He returned to the Pentagon in 1948 and remained there for the next thirteen years. White served successively as the legislative liaison, as a member of the Joint Strategic Survey Committee, and as deputy chief of staff for operations before becoming Twining's vice-chief of staff in June 1953.

When White became Chief of Staff in 1957, he selected the world renowned Curtis Lemay as his vice-chief of staff. Four years later, when White completed his term, Lemay was moved up to the Air Force's top position. For Lemay it marked the final achievement of a distinguished military career, which almost never was. Lemay did not graduate from West Point but from Ohio State. He wanted to attend the military academy but did not receive a congressional appointment. Still interested in a military career, Lemay joined the ROTC at Ohio State and was commissioned in 1928. One year later he completed flight training and was assigned to a fighter squadron. After serving with fighter units for seven years, he transferred to bombers. Prior to the outbreak of World War II, Lemay, who was an excellent navigator as well as an outstanding pilot, pioneered air routes over the North and South Atlantic.

After the outbreak of the war, Lemay organized the 305th Bombardment Group and led it into aerial combat in Europe in the autumn of 1942. This unit was one of the first bombardment units to enter combat and under Lemay's direction startled military strategists by not using evasive action on its bombing runs. In September 1943, at the age of thirty-seven, Lemay became the Army's youngest general and was placed in command of the 3rd Bombardment Division. As commanding officer of this unit, Lemay led the famed Regensberg raid, a B-17 shuttle mission that originated in England, struck deep in Germany, and terminated in Africa. In the summer of 1944, he was transferred to the Pacific, where he directed the 20th Bomber Command in the China-Burma-India theater. In early 1945 Lemay took over the 20th Air Force and personally led the low-level night-time incendiary attacks on Tokyo. Just before the end of the war, he yielded the 20th Air Force to Twining and became chief of staff for the U.S. strategic air forces in the Pacific.

After the war, Lemay spurned an offer from Ohio's Governor Frank Lausche to fill Ohio's vacant Senate seat and became deputy chief of staff for research and development. In late 1947, he was selected to be the commanding general of the American air forces in Europe and directed the Berlin Airlift. A year later, at the age of forty-two, Lemay became a full general and was named as the first head of the newly formed Strategic Air Command (SAC). Lemay developed SAC into such an efficient and reliable deterrent that Winston Churchill credited him with saving the Western World. After nine years at SAC, Lemay moved in as White's deputy.

Lemay served as the head of the Air Force for nearly the full four years. However, his longevity in office was more the result of political realities than his success as a military executive. After Lemay's first two years as Chief of Staff, the Kennedy administration wanted to replace him. But Lemay's term expired at the same time as that of CNO Anderson, who was also considered a liability. The President did not want to fire two chiefs at the same time, so he gave Lemay, who had more support in Congress than Anderson, a partial one-year reappointment. However, one year later, in the

summer of 1964, Lyndon Johnson was campaigning against Barry
Goldwater, and, in order to prevent Lemay from getting involved
in the campaign, his term was extended until after the election.
Thus, after three years and eight months as Chief of Staff, Lemay
was succeeded in January 1965 by John P. McConnell, who had
been vice-chief since August 1964.

John McConnell graduated from West Point in 1932, a classmate of General Earl Wheeler. Unlike most cadets, McConnell had
already graduated from college before he went to the military
academy. In his senior year at the military academy, McConnell
was selected to be first captain of the corps of cadets, West Point's
highest honor. He was commissioned directly into the Air Service
and received his wings in 1933. Prior to World War II, McConnell
served with a fighter squadron and in the training command. He
spent the first two years of the war in this country on the Air
Staff and in the training command. McConnell was assigned to
India in late 1943 and remained in that theater until the end of
hostilities, serving in various staff capacities.

After the war, McConnell, who was already a general officer,
spent two years in China as an air advisor to the Chinese government. He spent the period from 1947 to 1950 in the Pentagon.
For the next twelve years McConnell worked with the Strategic
Air Command in various capacities. He commanded two of SAC's
air forces, served as director of plans, and finally as vice-commander
in chief. In 1962 he was selected as Lemnitzer's deputy in Europe
and in August 1964 became Lemay's vice-chief.

McConnell served four and one-half years as Air Force Chief
of Staff. His second two-year term expired ten days after Richard
Nixon took office, and the chief executive waited for six months
before naming McConnell's vice-chief, John Ryan, to succeed him.
Ryan graduated from West Point in 1938 and received his pilot's
wings in 1939. He saw limited action in World War II, spending
most of the war in the training command. Ryan went to Europe
in early 1944, where he was the commander of a bomber group.

For the next twenty years Ryan spent his time working his way up to the top of the Strategic Air Command. He commanded two bomber wings, two divisions, and two of SAC's air forces. He also served as SAC's director of material and as vice-commander before becoming the head of SAC in December 1964. In those twenty years, Ryan's only assignment outside SAC was a one-year tour as Inspector General of the Air Force. After two years as commander of SAC, Ryan was named commander of all the air forces in the Pacific. He spent seventeen months in this position before moving up to vice-chief in August 1968.

After serving a four-year term as Air Force Chief of Staff, Ryan was succeeded by George Brown, the head of the Systems Command. Brown was the first officer to become Air Force Chief of Staff without having served first as vice-chief. Brown graduated from West Point in 1941 and became a pilot a year later. During World War II, he saw considerable action in Europe as part of the 93rd Bombardment Group, winning a Distinguished Service Cross and a Silver Star for daring raids behind enemy lines, including the famous low-level raid on the oil refineries at Ploesti, Rumania, on August 1, 1943, in which fifty-four planes were shot down.

For the next thirty years Brown's career was completely different from those of his predecessors. He attended the National War College and was associated with several types of aircraft commands, including tactical, transport, and intercepter. Brown spent seven years in the Pentagon but primarily in the joint arena. He was a military assistant to Secretaries of Defense Gates and McNamara, assistant to Chairman of the JCS Earl Wheeler, and headed a JCS unit designed to test weapon systems of all the military services. From August 1968 to September 1970, Brown commanded the 7th Air Force in Vietnam, and from September 1970 through August 1973 he was the commander of the Air Force Systems Command.

For two reasons, many people speculated, when Brown was appointed to the JCS, that he would soon move up from Air Force

Chief of Staff to chairman. First, it was the Air Force's "turn" to hold the top position. An Air Force officer had been chairman only three of the preceding twenty-five years. Second, Brown's previous experience in the joint arena seemed to make him well qualified for the chairmanship. Thus, it came as no surprise that when Moorer retired as chairman in the summer of 1974, Brown was named to succeed him. The only surprise was that Brown moved up so quickly. The expectation was that Moorer's term would be extended to allow Brown to serve at least two years as Air Force chief. However, Moorer's connection with the purloining of documents from the National Security Council by a Navy yeoman made him a political liability and his term was not extended. Thus, Brown became chairman after less than a year on the JCS.[13]

AIR FORCE: A COMPOSITE

The Air Force is composed of both flying and nonflying officers. The latter handle the support functions (for example, intelligence, administration) which are necessary for the conduct of flight operations. The flying officers are divided into pilots and nonpilots (navigators, bombardiers, etc.). Although any Air Force officer can serve as the Chief of Staff, all of the chiefs have been pilots. One nonflying officer did rise as high as vice-chief. William (Bozo) McKee, whose specialty was logistics, was Lemay's vice-chief from 1961 to 1964.

The Air Force was "granted its independence" from the Army by the same act which created the Department of Defense and the JCS. Therefore, each of the Air Force Chiefs of Staff has also been a member of the JCS. Table 8 contains a chronological list of these men with their pertinent background data.

Seven of the eight chiefs are graduates of the military academy at West Point. Curtis Lemay, who applied to the academy but was not appointed by his congressman, received his commission in

TABLE 8

Background Data on Air Force Chiefs of Staff

Name	Source & Year of Commission	Postgraduate	Age	Service	Years in Flag	4-Star	Tenure Years & Months	Post-C/S
Spaatz	USMA[a]—1914	CGS[b]	56	33	7	3	0 + 7	Retired
Vandenberg	USMA—1923	CGS AWC[c]	49	25	6	3	5 + 2	Retired
Twining	USMA—1918	CGS	56	35	11	3	4 + 0	Chairman
White	USMA—1920	CGS	55	37	15	4	4 + 0	Retired
Lemay	ROTC—1928	—	54	33	18	10	3 + 8	Fired
McConnell	USMA—1932	—	57	33	21	3	4 + 6	Retired
Ryan	USMA—1938	—	53	31	17	5	4 + 0	Retired
Brown	USMA—1941	National[d]	55	32	14	5	1 + 0	Chairman
Composite	USMA	CGS	54	33	14	5	3 + 9	Retired

[a] USMA—United States Military Academy
[b] CGS—Command and General Staff
[c] AWC—Army War College
[d] National—National War College

1928 from the Army ROTC at Ohio State. Since the Air Force
Academy did not begin operations until 1955, the Air Force's
future chiefs cannot come from its own academy until 1990 at the
earliest, and most of its leaders will continue to be products of an
Army school.

To date, postgraduate training at service schools has not been
particularly important in the careers of the Air Force chiefs. Three
of the last four chiefs have not attended any of the schools, and
only Vandenberg attended both a staff and a war college course.
However, this situation should change in the future. Many of the
chiefs were promoted so rapidly in World War II that they were
too high up in rank to attend a service school. For example, Lemay
and McConnell were lieutenants at the outbreak of World War II
and therefore too junior to attend the Staff College. However, when
the war ended, they were both flag officers and therefore too senior
for any of the war colleges at any level.

The average age of the Air Force chiefs at the time of their
selection is fifty-four. Hoyt Vandenberg, who took office three
months after his forty-ninth birthday, is the youngest man ever to
serve on the JCS. John McConnell, who had already graduated from
college before entering West Point, is the oldest man to take over
the Air Force's number one position. He was fifty-seven when he
succeeded Curtis Lemay in 1965. It took the eight chiefs an average of thirty-three years to climb the promotion ladder. Vandenberg's rise was the most rapid; the second Air Force Chief of Staff
succeeded Carl Spaatz after only twenty-five years of service.
Thomas White, who spent thirty-seven years in the service before
taking over in 1957, holds the distinction of being the chief with
the longest period of service. White, who became Chief of Staff
nine years after Vandenberg, graduated from West Point two years
ahead of Senator Arthur Vandenberg's famous nephew.

The average time that chiefs have spent as general officers is
fourteen years. As might be expected, Vandenberg spent the shortest time as a flag officer. He was elevated to the top spot six years

after making flag rank. John McConnell, who spent more than two-thirds of his military career as a flag officer before becoming chief, served the longest. All of the Air Force chiefs were already full generals before being selected and had spent an average of four years in that grade. All of the chiefs, except Lemay, spent approximately the same time as full generals. Lemay received his fourth star at the age of forty-two because of his accomplishments with the Strategic Air Command and had ten years in that status before being appointed to the JCS by John Kennedy.

Upon being selected as the first Air Force Chief of Staff, Carl Spaatz, who was exhausted by the rigors of World War II, agreed to serve only on an interim basis. After seven months President Truman appointed Hoyt Vandenberg as the first permanent Air Force Chief of Staff. The average time in office for Vandenberg and his six successors has been just under four years. Three of the chiefs have deviated slightly from the normal four-year tour, while one served less than a year. Vandenberg served just over five years and McConnell just over four years, while Lemay held office a little less than four years and Brown less than one year. Vandenberg and McConnell had their tours extended because of administration changes in the midst of ongoing wars. Lemay owed his unusual tour length to his support in Congress and in the Republican Party. Brown's short tour was occasioned by Moorer's difficulties.

Because of the rapid promotions of the Air Force chiefs during World War II, no clear pattern was developed for selection to flag officer. However, as indicated in table 9, after one becomes a general officer there are certain key positions in the operational and staff areas that lead to Chief of Staff. On the operational side there appear to be three stepping-stones to the top: command of an air force, an area command, and a type command. All eight of the chiefs have headed at least one air force and between them they have commanded nine different ones. Twining commanded three air forces, while White, McConnell, and Ryan each directed two.

TABLE 9

Career Patterns of Air Force Chiefs of Staff

Name	OPERATIONAL: COMMAND OF Air Force	Area	Type	STAFF Deputy	Vice
Spaatz	8 12	Africa	SAC[a]	Operations	2
Vandenberg	9	—	—	Intelligence	3
Twining	13 15 20	Alaskan	Material	Personnel	3
White	5 7	—	—	Operations	4
Lemay	20	European	SAC	Research & Development	4
McConnell	2 3	—	—	—	1
Ryan	2 16	Pacific	SAC	—	1
Brown	7	Vietnam	Systems	—	—

[a] SAC—Strategic Air Command

The 2nd and 20th Air Forces were each commanded by two different chiefs.

Five of the chiefs held Air Force area commands. Vandenberg, White, and McConnell never held an operational command above the level of the individual air force. However, both Vandenberg and McConnell were deputies to commanders in the European area, and White was chief of staff to the Pacific area commander. None of the five area commanders has headed the same section of the world. Spaatz commanded the air forces in Africa, Twining in Alaska, Lemay in Europe, Ryan in the Pacific, and Brown in Vietnam.

The five area commanders have also been type commanders, and three of these five type commanders have been in charge of the Strategic Air Command. Spaatz, Lemay, and Ryan were all SAC commanders, and McConnell was a SAC vice-commander. Brown and Twining, the only Air Force officers to move up to chairman, came to the JCS from the Systems Command and Material Command, respectively.

In the staff area, the single most important position has been vice-chief of staff. Prior to the appointment of George Brown in August 1973, every chief had served as vice-chief of staff immediately prior to moving to the top. Moreover, some of these men served in the Air Force's number two position for considerable periods of time. Both White and Lemay were the number two man for four-year periods, while Twining and Vanderberg occupied the position for three years. Service as a deputy chief used to be quite necessary. The first five chiefs had also been deputies in different areas. However, none of the past three leaders had ever seen service on the deputy level. George Brown came from a different mold than most of his predecessors. He has spent his operational career in the nonstrategic area and his staff service in the joint arena as assistant to both the chairman of the JCS and the Secretary of Defense.

CHAIRMEN: THE INDIVIDUALS

All of the chairmen except Arthur Radford served first as a service chief. Radford came to the chairmanship directly from an operational command. Radford graduated from the Naval Academy in 1916, in a class that also produced two other men who would become members of the JCS, Admirals Fechteler and Carney, and a total of forty admirals. After graduation, Radford served with the battleship *South Carolina* in the Atlantic during World War I. When the war ended, he entered flight training and was designated as an aviator in 1921. Before Pearl Harbor, Radford alternated between sea duty with aviation units and shore duty in the Navy's Bureau of Aeronautics. In the early days of the war, he was the director of aviation training for the Navy. From September 1943 to April 1944 he was in command of a carrier task group that operated against the Japanese on Baker, Makin, and Tarawa. After six months in Washington as assistant to the deputy CNO for Air, Radford returned to the Pacific as commander of Carrier Division 6 for the remainder of the war.

After the war, Radford served for fourteen months as deputy CNO for Air and then took command of the 2nd Fleet. In January 1948, he was appointed by Denfeld as vice-chief of naval operations. While in this position he led the "revolt of the admirals" against Denfeld's decision to acquiesce in the cancellation of the supercarrier *United States*. When Denfeld was fired, Radford was exiled to the Pacific and made CINCPACFLT. However, the outbreak of the Korean War shifted the nation's attention to the Pacific, brought Radford back into the limelight and to the attention of Secretary of Defense Wilson. During Eisenhower's famous preinauguration visit to Korea on board the cruiser *Helena*, the newly-elected President met with Radford and approved him as chairman of the JCS. Although Radford wanted to be Chief of Naval Operations, he agreed to become chairman because he felt that he, like Bradley, would receive a fifth star. Radford served four years as chairman, and when it became clear that he would not receive his fifth star, he refused Eisenhower's offer of an extension and retired in 1957.

CHAIRMEN: A COMPOSITE

The law specifies that a uniformed officer of any military service may be appointed chairman of the JCS. Thus far, only representatives of the Army, Navy, and Air Force have been selected, and in view of its comparatively small size, it is unlikely that someone from the Marine Corps will be selected in the future. Since the creation of the position of chairman in 1949, an Army officer has occupied it for more than half of the intervening years, that is, fourteen years. As indicated in table 10, four of the eight appointees have been Army generals, while only two Navy aviators and two Air Force officers have held the post. There are no statutes mandating the rotation of the position among the services. President Eisenhower thought that rotation was a good idea and appointed an officer from each of the services during his eight years in office. Presidents Kennedy and Johnson appointed only Army officers, while President Nixon apparently reinstituted the rotation pattern by appointing a Navy and an Air Force officer to this nation's highest military position.[14]

The average age of the eight chairmen is just under fifty-eight years, and there is very little deviation among the appointees. Wheeler, at fifty-six, was the youngest selectee, and Lemnitzer, who

TABLE 10

Selective Information on Chairmen of the JCS

Name	Service	Age	Time As Service Chief	Tenure	Post-CJCS
Bradley	Army	56	1 + 6	4 + 0	Retired
Radford	Navy	57	—	4 + 0	Retired
Twining	Air Force	59	4 + 0	3 + 2	Sick
Lemnitzer	Army	61	1 + 2	2 + 0	NATO
Taylor	Army	60	4 + 0	1 + 9	Ambassador
Wheeler	Army	56	1 + 11	6 + 0	Retired
Moorer	Navy	58	3 + 0	4 + 0	Retired
Brown	Air Force	56	1 + 0		
Composite	Army	58	2 + 1	3 + 7	Retired

was the oldest man to become a service chief, is also the oldest man to be appointed chairman. He was sixty-one when he was unexpectedly tapped for the post because of Twining's sudden illness. All of the chairmen, except Arthur Radford, had previous experience as a service chief, and all of the service chiefs except Taylor moved up to the chairmanship directly from that position. Taylor retired in 1959 and was out of government for two years. After the Bay of Pigs fiasco, Kennedy became disenchanted with his Joint Chiefs and appointed Taylor as his special assistant for military affairs. One year later, in October 1962, Kennedy selected the scholarly soldier to replace Lemnitzer as chairman. Radford was a likely candidate for CNO until he led the "revolt of the admirals" in 1949.

Most of the chairmen did not get to serve their full time as service chief before moving up to the chairmanship. Their average time as service chief was only two years and one month. Twining and Taylor were the only chairmen to complete a full term as service chief, and, as was discussed above, Taylor did not move directly to the top position. Lemnitzer and Brown had very short tenures as a service chief. Lemnitzer had served only fourteen months when General Twining's illness left the post vacant, while Brown was tapped for the top spot after less than a year on the JCS when Moorer's activities made him a political liability. The average term in office for a chairman has been just over three and a half years. Three men have served less than the normal four-year term. Twining resigned for health reasons after three years. Lemnitzer was "kicked upstairs" to NATO after completion of his first term so that Taylor's role as the President's principal military advisor could be legitimized by making him chairman, and Taylor himself resigned after twenty-one months to take over the embassy in Saigon. Bradley, Radford, and Moorer served two complete two-year tours before stepping down. Wheeler, the only chief with significant staff and joint experience before his JCS appointment, was apparently the most successful chairman. He was appointed three times by Lyndon Johnson and once by Richard Nixon and served a total of six years.

A COMPARISON

The preceding analysis has indicated some distinctive differences in the backgrounds and career patterns among the men who rise to the top in each service. The information for each of the services is summarized in table 11. As indicated therein, the "naval aristocracy" has never admitted a non-Annapolis graduate into its highest echelon, while Army and Air Force each have allowed one maverick to become its Chief of Staff. The Army has provided its future leaders with far more postgraduate training than the other services. All of the Army's leaders have attended the two senior service schools, while only half of the Navy and Air Force chiefs have attended one of the service colleges.

The average age and length of service is slightly different for each of the services. The Army's average in both categories is slightly higher because they have not yet had an "under fifty whiz kid," like Vandenberg or Zumwalt, rise to the top. Time in flag and time as a four-star general officer has been considerably shorter for CNOs because the Navy does not have a one-star general officer rank, and three CNOs have been "deep-selected" (that is, chosen from below the normal zone from which chiefs are normally chosen) as opposed to one in the Army and none in the Air Force. Chiefs of Staff of the Air Force have remained in office much longer because only one has moved up to chairman during his tenure, none has died in office, and the only Air Force chief who was fired was retained almost the full four years for reasons of political expediency.

Operational command billets have been important stepping-stones in all three services. The Army's Harold Johnson is the only post–World War II chief to rise to the top without having held at least one major command as a flag officer. As indicated in table 11, the great majority of the chiefs have held command at three

TABLE 11

*A Summary of the Background
Characteristics of the Joint Chiefs of Staff*

ITEM	SERVICE			
	Army	*Navy*	*Air Force*	*Composite*
Academy Graduates	90%	100%	87%	92%
Service Schools Attended: 1	100%	55%	50%	68%
2	100%	11%	12%	31%
Civilian Postgraduate	20%	10%	—	7%
Age	55	54	54	54
Years of:				
Service	34	33	33	33
Flag	12	7	14	11
4 Stars	4	3	4	4
Four-Star Selectees	90%	55%	100%	82%
Tenure	2 + 6	2 + 10	3 + 9	3 + 0
Chairmen	4	2	2	3
Operational Experience				
Level 1	90%	88%	100%	93%
Level 2	70%	56%	62%	63%
Level 3	70%	78%	62%	70%
Staff				
Deputy	70%	22%	62%	51%
Vice	40%	0	75%	38%

levels before assuming their positions as service leaders.[15] Prior experience as a deputy and vice-chief has been important in both the Army and the Air Force, but of very little significance in the Navy.

But, more important, the preceding analysis indicates that small groups of individuals are carefully groomed by the services for the top position after they reach the 0-6 level. The individuals are combat-oriented line officers, usually distinguished graduates of the respective military academies, who have performed well in a variety of assignments. Career patterns prior to the 0-6 level (colonel or captain) do not seem particularly important and vary a great deal among the future chiefs. Bradley spent his mid-career years in schools while Lemnitzer was in the field. Moorer spent a great deal of time in the Pentagon while Anderson's mid-career was at sea. Ryan spent his mid-years in the Strategic Air Command while Brown was in the Pentagon. But, from the 0-6 level on up, each of the services usually makes sure that its future leaders spend some time in certain key assignments. Likewise, conspicuous gallantry on the battlefield does not seem particularly important. Several of the chiefs were highly decorated, while others earned little more than combat ribbons.

Potential Army Chiefs of Staff must pass through the Staff and War College system prior to flag selection. As general officers, the future chiefs are given command at the division, corps, and area levels, particularly in areas of hot combat, and are assigned to the Pentagon on the Army Staff. Even Earl Wheeler, who had made a brilliant reputation as a staff officer, had to be moved out of the Pentagon for short tours as commander of the 2nd Armored Division and III Infantry Corps, and as deputy commander in Europe, so that he could complete the grooming process.

Future Navy leaders must be naval academy graduates but need not be concerned with school as staff assignments. However, prospective CNOs must command at least one large surface ship prior to selection to admiral. After selection, the Navy chief must fly his flag at sea as the commander of a division or force of ships and an entire fleet. In order to prepare George Anderson for the Navy's top position, the Navy reverted him from three to two stars to allow him to serve as commander of Carrier Division 6, a traditional stepping-stone to CNO for naval aviators. The Air Force grooms certain of its pilots to be its future leaders by placing them in charge of an air force, an area command, and a type command, and by seeing that they serve as deputy and vice-chiefs of staff. Even Curtis Lemay, who virtually created the Strategic Air Command, was taken from this prestigious position and placed in the Pentagon as vice-chief of staff so that he would be in line to step in when Thomas White retired.

In his study of the military leadership of 1950, Morris Janowitz[16] found that the majority of the elite nucleus of the services had followed adaptive or individualist career patterns. On the surface, this would seem to contradict our findings about the career patterns of the JCS. However, this is not the case. Janowitz's findings are consistent with those discussed above. His elite nucleus consists of those who reach the two-star level. Our study is primarily concerned about what happens to officers after they reach that level. Moreover, Janowitz's adaptive or individualist career pattern consists of unique assignments early in a military career, while our focus has been on the last one-third of an officer's career where the officer is groomed for Chief of Staff. Finally, Janowitz admits that even those in the adaptive career patterns have had the essential elements of the prescribed career (for example, war college training), and this has been our conclusion.

Our study demonstrates how successful the services have been in establishing the field from which the chiefs are chosen. As is indicated in table 11, 82 percent of those selected for the JCS have already been four-star officers, and in only one case, Arleigh Burke, has a man who was below the top 10 percent of the flag officers been selected as chief. However, this does not mean that the service always gets a particular man. Admiral McDonald may have handpicked Admiral Moorer as his successor, but Moorer was not able to prevent Melvin Laird from selecting the young, outspoken surface officer, Admiral Zumwalt to be his successor. Vandenberg, Twining, White, Lemay, and McConnell were successful in getting their type of man on the JCS, but John Ryan could not pass the torch to General Meyer, the head of SAC and his former vice-chief. However, Moorer and Ryan could not be completely unhappy with their successors. The Navy had deep-selected Zumwalt for rear admiral and the Air Force had already elevated Brown to the four-star level. From the service perspective these appointments were simply premature.

As a result of this grooming process by the services, there are certain similarities exhibited by all the officers who are selected for membership on the JCS. Over 90 percent of the chiefs are products of either West Point or Annapolis. At the time that these men attended the academies, these institutions had only a narrow, single-track technical curriculum almost devoid of socio-humanistic electives. Subsequent to graduating from either the military or naval academy, more than one-third never received additional education. Of the approximately 65 percent who did spend at least one year in a postgraduate environment, nearly all spent it at one of the military's own colleges. Arleigh Burke and William Westmoreland are the only members of the JCS to do postgraduate work at a civilian university, and only Burke has a masters degree.

All of the chiefs are combat-oriented line officers whose main accomplishment has been demonstrated expertise in the weapons of violence peculiar to their own services. It is ironic that no staff officer in the military has ever risen or can rise to be Chief of Staff. Only Earl Wheeler and George Brown have had extensive joint or staff assignments. The Air Force has refused to allow line officers who are not pilots to acceed to their top position. Very few of the CNOs have spent much time in Washington after their selection to flag rank. Army Chiefs of Staff come to the Pentagon direct from the battlefront.

Finally, all of the chiefs must spend a considerable period of time working their way up the service bureaucracy. The typical chief is in his mid-fifties and has spent about four years as a full general or admiral, eleven years as a flag officer, and thirty-three years in his service before appointment to the top position. Only Admiral Zumwalt and General Vandenberg reached the JCS before their fiftieth birthdays or with less than thirty years of service, and only five officers were not full generals or admirals at the time of appointment.

Thus, it should come as no surprise that civilian superiors have found that the typical chief is unable or unwilling to rise above the narrow parochial interests of his own service in particular, or those of the Pentagon in general. He is a product of a nearly forty-year socialization process and has had limited exposure to a nonmilitary or even a nonservice environment. With some exceptions, his career has followed a specific pattern laid out by his service, particularly after he has been selected for flag officer. Moreover, the only constituency he has had to satisfy in his entire career is the selection board composed of members of his own service.

Let us now turn to an analysis of how these individuals who have been pushed to the top perform when they get there. In chapter three we will examine the performance of the Joint Chiefs of Staff in the annual budgetary wars and in chapter four their performance during the wars in Vietnam and Korea.

CHAPTER THREE

★

The Battle
of the Potomac

INTRODUCTION

Military or defense policy making is essentially a political process. That military policy is not, as some might imagine, the result of deductions from national policy or foreign policy or national security policy, but rather the product of a competition among individuals and groups, a product of the normal political processes by which American domestic policy is produced, has been shown by the work of the Institute of War and Peace Studies.[1] Aaron Wildavsky has convincingly demonstrated that even in the area of national defense, policy making and politics are synonymous.[2]

The making of military policy may be divided into four phases: planning for the use of force; budgeting, or the request and approval of funds to procure material to implement the plans: procurement; and operations. While each phase is important and all the phases are to some extent interdependent, the second phase is of overriding importance. If the necessary funds are not requested and/or granted, the proper mix of men and material cannot be procured and the plans cannot be implemented.

Scholars, statesmen, and military leaders have been unanimous in pointing out the importance of the defense budget for military policy. The first Secretary of Defense, James Forrestal, called the budget the key to a sound defense policy.[3] Robert McNamara referred to the budget as a quantitative expression of operating plans.[4] General Omar Bradley, the first chairman of the JCS, stated that in the final analysis the budget controls military policy.[5] Senator Richard Russell referred to the defense budget as the "moment of truth" when it is decided what emphasis will be placed on each of the several kinds of forces that constitute the military power of the United States.[6] Arthur Smithies, well known economist, pointed out that defense policy does not become crystallized until budgetary decisions are taken, and that although strategy may be determined outside the budgetary process, the complexion of defense policy changes radically depending upon whether $25 billion, $50 billion, or $75 billion a year is spent for defense.[7] Political scientist Bernard Gordon summed up the importance of the defense budget most succinctly when he said, "To a degree not paralleled in any other field, in defense, dollars are policy."[8]

Because of the political nature of military policy making and the importance of the budgetary process to military policy, none of the functions performed by the JCS is more important than the part it plays in the budgetary process. If the principal spokesmen for the military point of view within the American government do not play their proper role in the budgetary process, the results may be catastrophic for the American political system.

The defense budget process is the entire chain of events that decides how much money will be allotted to defense and to what functions it will be allocated. There are two clearly defined phases within this process: executive preparation and submission of the defense budget to the Congress, and legislative authorization and appropriation of funds. As principal military advisors to both the executive and legislative branches of government, the Joint Chiefs are intimately involved in both phases.

Each post–World War II President has developed his own mode of formulating the annual federal budget, and within the Department of Defense each Secretary of Defense has developed a particular style of producing the defense budget. Moreover, each administration has had a particular expectation about the proper role that the JCS ought to play in both the legislative and the executive phases of the defense budget process. This chapter will analyze the JCS within the context of the expectations of each administration.

THE TRUMAN ADMINISTRATION

The JCS was created in time to be involved with the last four defense budgets produced by the Truman administration, from fiscal year 1950 to fiscal year 1953. During these four budget evolutions, the JCS worked with no less than four Secretaries of Defense: James Forrestal, Louis Johnson, George Marshall, and Robert Lovett. Moreover, these budgets were produced in two entirely different environments.

The 1950 and 1951 budgets were produced in an environment characterized by a severe decline in military preparedness and a deterioration in the relationships between the United States and the Soviet Union and among the three services. From a World War II high of $81.5 billion in 1945, defense spending had dropped to about $10 billion by fiscal year 1949. World War II cooperation between the U.S. and the U.S.S.R. had degenerated into a cold war between the superpowers after the fall of Czechoslovakia in 1948. Interservice cooperation during World War II had floundered in the postwar period upon the rocks of unification and differing views over the course of future conflicts.

On the other hand, the last two budgets of the Truman administration were produced during the Korean War. The North Korean attack, which occurred about one week after the approval of a very austere 1951 budget, reversed the decline in defense spending, hardened the nation's view toward the U.S.S.R. and all other Communist nations, and brought about a submergence of service rivalries.

Because of the newness of the Department of Defense, the frequent change of secretaries, and the volatility of the international environment, no clear pattern of budget making emerged in the Truman administration. Therefore, let us look at the role played by the JCS under each secretary individually.

PRE-KOREAN WAR

Secretaries of Defense James Forrestal and Louis Johnson split the thirty-six months between the creation of the Department of Defense and the outbreak of the Korean War almost evenly. Forrestal served ten days more than eighteen months and Johnson nine days less. Although each worked within the same environment, their modi operandi and relationships with the JCS were quite different.

James Forrestal worked with five military chiefs on two budgetary evolutions, a supplement to the 1949 budget and the 1950 budget. In each of these evolutions, the Joint Chiefs played similar roles. The Secretary of Defense received definitive ceilings from the Bureau of the Budget. He communicated these ceilings to the Joint Chiefs and asked them to produce a budget within these ceilings. The chiefs submitted budgets to him that were well in excess of the ceiling because they could not agree on where to reduce the individual service budgets. Each chief was willing to cut the total package if the majority of the cuts came from the other services. Their budget submissions to Forrestal were simply the sum of the three individual service budgets. In 1949, the chiefs asked for a $9 billion supplement and in 1950 they requested a total budget of $29.4 billion. The ceilings for these budgets were $3 billion and $15 billion, respectively.[9]

Forrestal sought assistance from two outside sources to bridge the gap, but neither helped. He created a board of non-JCS officers to reduce the budget, but it made only a small reduction. He then asked the Secretary of State to provide guidance to the Joint Chiefs to enable them to adjust the world situation to administration ceilings, but Secretary Marshall refused. Forrestal succeeded in bridging the gap through personal diplomacy. He summoned the chiefs to his office and told them that they could not have satisfactory and usable military power under the budgetary limitations, but that if they would produce a budget in the vicinity of the President's ceilings, he would make further attempts to get the President to raise the limitations somewhat. For him to present the chiefs' original estimates to the administration would strain both his and their credibility, but if they came close to the budget ceilings, he could tell the President they were not taking his decision lightly. The chiefs cooperated, but the White House did not. In fiscal year 1949 the chiefs and Forrestal agreed on a $3.48 billion supplement and in fiscal year 1950 they settled on $16.9 billion. Forrestal made impassioned pleas to the White House, but Truman refused to raise the ceilings on either occasion. The secretary also arranged for the Joint Chiefs to plead their case directly with the chief executive, but the result was still the same.[10]

Although there was no prior experience concerning the role that the JCS would play in the executive phase of the budget process, and the 1947 legislation was vague on the subject, Forrestal's perception of the appropriate role for the chiefs was quite clear. He expected them to advise him on the division of funds within the limitations of the President's ceilings and thus share responsibility with him for the division.[11] The JCS was primarily service oriented. Each chief viewed his primary responsibility as protecting the interests of his own branch. He realized that defense spending was limited, but felt that he could not take responsibility for any reductions that might involve his service. If cuts had to be made, each chief favored letting the other services bear the brunt, or forcing the Secretary of Defense or the President to make the reductions.[12]

Both President Truman and Secretary Forrestal made it clear to the JCS what role they expected the chiefs to play before the Congress. In May 1948, when Truman made his decisions on the ceilings for the 1949 supplement and the 1950 defense budget, he informed the Joint Chiefs that he expected them to support the ceilings publicly and privately. Forrestal reinforced the President's demands by sending a memorandum to the chiefs directing them to keep their differences within the family. The secretary added that if any chief felt he could not do so when testifying before the Congress, he ought to resign.[13]

Despite these directives, the chiefs were quite outspoken before the Congress during Forrestal's tenure. Air Force Chiefs of Staff Spaatz and Vandenberg argued against the administration's balanced force posture and urged Congress to provide funds for fifteen additional air groups for the Air Force.[14] Army Chief of Staff Bradley urged Congress to transfer the funds Forrestal had provided for naval aviation to the Air Force.[15] CNO Denfeld complained that the administration placed too much emphasis on the Air Force's strategic mission.[16] The chiefs' testimony to the Congress was supported by the service secretaries. Air Force Secretary Stuart Symington was particularly outspoken in his criticism of the policies of Forrestal.

Louis Johnson assumed the helm at the Pentagon while Congress was hearing testimony on the budget for fiscal year 1950 and the Joint Chiefs were working on a statement of forces and major national requirements that would provide a foundation for a 1951 budget of less than $15 billion. Johnson did not wait long to make his impact felt on either budget. Within a few weeks of his appointment he boasted to the Senate Subcommittee on Military Appropriations that he could save a billion dollars in the Department of Defense by cutting out waste, duplications, and unnecessary civilian employment. Obviously impressed, the Senate gave him authority to reduce expenditures by $434 million.[17] On April 23, 1949, within a month after succeeding Forrestal and less than a week after the Navy had completed well publicized keel-laying ceremonies, Johnson cancelled construction of the $500 million, 65,000-ton, flush deck supercarrier, the *United States*. This was done despite the fact that the Navy already had $364 million invested in it and Congress had appropriated funds for the ship for two consecutive fiscal years.

In June, the budget director informed the secretary that the budgetary ceiling for 1951 would be 1.5 million less than for 1950, or $13.5 billion. Without asking the services for the implications of the budget cut on their programs, Johnson then ordered a reduction in 1950 expenditures of approximately $1 billion and directed the JCS to agree on a budget for 1951 below $13.5 billion or face the prospect of an across-the-board reduction by him. On two occasions during the summer of 1949, President Truman met with Johnson and the chiefs to discuss the adequacy of the ceiling. On both occasions the secretary and the chiefs assured the President that $13.5 billion was more than sufficient.[18] The service budgets which the chiefs submitted to Johnson amounted to $13.31 billion. Johnson cut about $120 million of "fat" from the budget and sent it to the White House. The Bureau of the Budget reduced this figure by another $1 billion before finalizing it. The Joint Chiefs accepted both reductions without complaint and then proceeded to defend the $12.2 billion budget vigorously before a stunned Congress which wondered how military experts could support a 20 percent decline in defense spending while the international situation was rapidly worsening.

There is little doubt about the role that Johnson perceived for himself. His primary job was to bring about economy in the Pentagon. Johnson saw himself as the President's representative to the Department of Defense enforcing the administration's will on an avaricious military. Johnson would not think of attempting to get the White House to raise the budget ceilings, but he took every opportunity to reduce spending levels in the Pentagon; for example, he seized upon a technicality to split the JCS and cancel the super-carrier. Johnson's conception of the appropriate role for the JCS followed from the conception of his own job. He expected the chiefs to divide the funds voluntarily within the ceilings imposed from above. If the chiefs could not get together voluntarily, Johnson felt that that was their problem. He would capitalize on their splits to reduce expenditures, or he would simply order across-the-board cuts.

Johnson's actions put the fear of God into the Joint Chiefs and made them real team players. They refused to challenge the budgetary ceilings in two meetings with Truman and they supported the budget before Congress. Army Chief Collins actually tried to demonstrate to Congress that the Army contributed more to the nation's security with less men. Chairman Bradley told Congress that the military would be doing a disservice to the country if they recommended higher defense budgets.[19] However, CNO Louis Denfeld proved to be the ultimate team player. When Johnson canceled the supercarrier, Secretary of the Navy Sullivan resigned in protest and most of the Navy's senior officer corps were outraged. Denfeld not only accepted the Secretary of Defense's decision, but urged his fellow officers to do the same. Many senior officers refused to accept Denfeld's advice and repudiated his leadership. They rallied around vice-CNO Admiral Radford, and retired naval heroes such as Halsey and Nimitz, and publicly attacked the policy of relying solely on the Air Force's B-36 bomber for our strategic capability and thereby denying a role for carrier aviation in the strategic arena. In press conferences, radio appearances, magazine articles, and with leaked documents, naval officers called the B-36 a "billion dollar blunder," claimed that Navy jets could easily shoot it down, and accused senior defense officials of personal corruption in the B-36 production process. The publicity generated by these wild charges led to demands for a congressional inquiry into the issue. Denfeld attempted to curtail the inquiry but was not successful. The House Armed Services Committee held lengthy hearings, and the Navy case was argued primarily by Admiral Arthur Radford and by then Captain Arleigh Burke, head of the organizational policy and research division. Radford presented the arguments against the B-36 and Burke defended the carrier. In spite of the hearings, Congress did not attempt to change Johnson's decision. But the episode, which became known as the "revolt of the admirals," cost "team player" Denfeld his job.[20]

THE KOREAN WAR

By early September, 1950, the United States was very close to being driven off the Korean peninsula by a small Asian nation, and the public, demanding to know how this could happen to a superpower, was looking for scapegoats. Since the President and the Joint Chiefs of Staff could hardly be removed in the midst of a war, Louis Johnson, the apostle of economy, was fired and the organizer of victory in World War II, George Marshall, was named to succeed him. Marshall presided over the Pentagon for only one year. During this time, Marshall and the Joint Chiefs worked on the problem of mobilizing the United States for war. They produced a defense budget for fiscal year 1952 that increased defense spending by 458 percent over fiscal year 1951 levels and raised the level of manpower in the Department of Defense from 2.2 million to nearly 5 million. While Marshall was Secretary of Defense, there were no real budgetary constraints, nor were there any complaints to the Congress. The only real constraints on defense spending were the needs of the troops in the field on the Korean peninsula and the limitations on the speed with which weapons and munitions could be produced and force levels raised.

Robert Lovett succeeded Marshall in September 1951 and worked with the chiefs on the last budget of the Truman administration, the fiscal year 1953 budget. The starting point for this budget was a force level estimate made by the JCS. These estimates were approved by the National Security Council one month after Lovett took office. However, when these estimates were costed out, they came to $71 billion and Secretary Lovett directed the JCS to prepare alternative force levels that could be accommodated within a ceiling of $45 billion. After analyzing both budgets, Lovett and the Joint Chiefs agreed to a compromise budget of $55 billion. This was the same figure that Marshall and the JCS had arrived at in fiscal year 1952. When the Bureau of the Budget and the President reduced this compromise figure by $3 billion, both the secretary and the JCS protested strenuously. Despite their arguments, the President held firm and presented a $52 billion defense budget to Congress.[21]

The bulk of the testimony of the secretary and the JCS before Congress on the 1953 budget was devoted to supporting the budget and defending the assumptions of the administration's limited war policy. Despite JCS pleas, the Congress, which was becoming frustrated by the apparent indecisiveness of the war in Korea and which was gearing up for the 1952 election campaign, reduced the budget by almost 10 percent. Moreover, many Republicans and conservative Democrats complained that the Joint Chiefs had become too closely identified with the partisan policies of the Truman administration and demanded that President Eisenhower replace them en masse. As Senator Robert Taft put it, "I have come to the point where I do not accept them as experts."[22] Ironically, after Forrestal's resignation, Truman's chiefs had come to play the part in the budget envisioned for them by the administration, and for their reward they would leave office soon after he did.

THE EISENHOWER
ADMINISTRATION

A great many changes took place at home and abroad during the Eisenhower years. For the purpose of strengthening the secretary vis-à-vis the JCS, the Department of Defense was reorganized in 1953 and in 1958. The Korean War ended and a "new look" at military strategy produced a policy of massive retaliation. The "Great Equation"[23] replaced Truman's budgetary ceilings. Joseph Stalin died and the cold war was succeeded by peaceful coexistence. The Soviet Union developed an H-bomb well ahead of the predicted date and also drew first blood in the space race.

Dwight Eisenhower appointed three men as his Secretary of Defense. His first appointee, Charles Wilson, held office for nearly five years. Wilson's successor, Neil McElroy, served two years, and the last appointee, Thomas Gates, only one. During the first year of the Republican administration, Eisenhower and Wilson developed an orderly defense budget process which remained stable for the entire eight years.

The production of the defense budget within the executive under Eisenhower usually took an entire calendar year.[24] The process was initiated about eighteen months before the fiscal year in which the budget was to be effective and twelve months before the budget was to be submitted to the Congress. For example, work on the budget for fiscal year 1957, which was to be submitted to Congress in January 1956 and which would become effective on July 1, 1956, began in January 1955 and lasted until December of that year.

The process was inaugurated in January when the National Security Council produced the Basic National Security Policy (BNSP). This document was intended to be a comprehensive statement of American strategic policy and had as one of its main purposes providing guidance for the Joint Chiefs in planning for force and weapon levels. Although the Security Council devoted a great deal of time and energy to the drafting of the BNSP, the document was useless for budgeting purposes. Rather than resolving the sharp differences of opinion over what the strategic policy of the United States should be, the council glossed over them to make the document acceptable to all parties. It meant all things to all men and settled nothing. For example, the 1958 edition stated that the United States would depend upon the weapons of mass retaliation, but at the same time maintain flexible forces capable of coping with a lesser situation.[25]

After completion, the Basic National Security Policy was sent to the JCS to serve as a guide for their Joint Strategic Operations Plan (JSOP). The JSOP is a document of many volumes that prescribes the forces that the Joint Chiefs believe are required to carry out military strategy and national objectives. Because the Basic Security Policy could be interpreted in so many ways, each service chief stressed that portion of the policy that enhanced the primary mission of his service. Consequently, the JSOP was really three separate plans added together and called a joint plan.[26] Secretary of Defense Wilson tried on several occasions to get the JCS to produce a joint plan, but to no avail. Consequently, he was forced to rely on Admiral Radford, the chairman of the JCS, and on his own staff (the Office of the Secretary of Defense) for most of the force level planning. On one occasion, he even produced his own long-range plan for force levels.[27] The completed Joint Strategic Operations Plan was sent to the services in late June. It was intended to serve as a guide or framework for the individual military departments in the production of their separate budgets.

While the Joint Chiefs were completing work on the Operations Plan, the National Security Council was deciding upon a ceiling for defense expenditures for the next fiscal year. The ceiling was obtained by estimating total income, subtracting the projected expenditures of all other government agencies, and then allocating the remainder to defense.[28] The object was a balanced budget in every fiscal year, and not even such crises as Sputnik or Suez could alter that objective.[29] The remainder for defense usually came to between 9 and 10 percent of the gross national product. The defense ceiling was transmitted to the service chiefs by the chairman in midsummer.

The individual service budgets were submitted to the JCS in

September. The Joint Chiefs were supposed to review the budgets for conformity with the Basic National Security Policy and the Joint Strategic Operations Plan. The defense secretary expected the chiefs to produce a total defense budget which conformed as closely as possible to the plans but did not exceed the ceiling. However, the service budgets exceeded the ceiling by an average of 15 percent.[30] Not once did these JCS-approved budgets come reasonably close to the ceiling. On three occasions, the budget requests exceeded the ceiling by more than 20 percent. The JCS refused to trim the budgets. Because of the vagueness of the Basic Security Policy and the ambivalence of the Joint Operations Plan, the chiefs could and did justify every item in the service budgets and refused to make reductions on the grounds of national security. Moreover, there was still a great deal of bitterness among the services and any attempt by a service chief to acquiesce in cuts for his service would be looked upon as near treason by his subordinates. Wilson and McElroy tried a variety of approaches to induce the JCS to scale down these requests. These approaches ranged from direct commands to subtle hints, but always had the same lack of results.

In Eisenhower's first year in office, 1953, Wilson twice directed the Joint Chiefs to indicate where reductions could be made in the services' $37.82 billion request to bring it under $35 billion. The JCS refused to follow either directive on the ground that any reduction would increase the danger to national security. The following year Wilson directed Chairman Arthur Radford to persuade the chiefs to make the desired reductions. Radford was unable to get the chiefs to agree on a lower level of expenditures and was forced to make recommendations for reductions himself.[31]

Four years later, when he was faced with a JCS-approved budget of $44.67 billion and an administration ceiling of $38 billion, Secretary Neil McElroy tried a more subtle approach than had his predecessors. He asked the chiefs how they would divide $38 billion, without in any way implying that this was the amount they approved. The chiefs discussed this hypothetical question briefly and then informed McElroy that they unanimously agreed on how to split up $34 billion, but each chief felt he needed the additional $4 billion for his own service and could not voluntarily give it away to another military department.[32] In essence, they were telling the Secretary that they needed the entire $45 billion. In 1959, Eisenhower intervened personally by inviting the chiefs to a stag dinner at the White House. During the dinner, the former general gave the chiefs a pep talk on the great need for more cooperation on their part with the secretary in connection with the budget. Only Chairman Twining was receptive. The chiefs refused to change their behavior.[33]

So little did the Joint Chiefs have to do with the final defense budget that they never even considered such important questions as the size of the Army, the number of aircraft carriers, or the amount of deterrent forces. The job of making such important decisions, and therefore where to make the major reductions, was left to the office of the Secretary of Defense and to the President. Wilson and McElroy often ordered across-the-board reductions. The comptroller for the Department of Defense, Wilfred McNeil, made most of the detailed decisions. Eisenhower made about fifteen major budgetary decisions annually and was the chief architect of the plan for reducing the Army's ground forces.[34]

The Eisenhower administration expected the Joint Chiefs to cooperate fully with the defense office and to act with that office as a single staff for the Secretary of Defense. The defense secretaries did not want purely military advice from the JCS. They expected the chiefs to broaden their outlooks to include a wide range of domestic and international economic and political factors.[35] The majority of the chiefs felt that their primary duties were to provide military advice and to protect the vested interests of their services. The chiefs felt that neither their military professionalism nor their service interests could be well protected by taking into account political and economic criteria. They resisted all attempts to get them to color their advice. Consequently, they had neither a harmonious relationship with the administration nor a large impact in the budget process.

Dwight Eisenhower, the career soldier, made it perfectly clear to every member of the JCS whom he appointed that he expected the JCS to support his yearly defense budget before the Congress. He made it obvious that he would consider anything less than enthusiastic support for his budgets as an act of disloyalty to the Commander in Chief. So confident was Eisenhower that the JCS would obey this direct order that, without consulting the chiefs, he announced to the Congress upon submitting his first defense budget that it had the unanimous approval of the JCS.[36]

For the first two years of his administration, Eisenhower's order was followed. In 1953 and 1954 Ridgway came very close to contesting Eisenhower's "massive retaliation" strategy before Congress but always refrained from open criticism and saved his true feelings until after his retirement in 1955. However, from 1955 on, all of the chiefs, except the chairman, took great exception to Eisenhower's budgets. Maxwell Taylor and Arleigh Burke were particularly outspoken in their criticism of the "New Look," the sloppy directives, and the stringent budget ceilings. Taylor told the Congress that the policies embodied by the Eisenhower defense budgets actually jeopardized national security. In his view, American atomic power had not been enough to keep the peace, as evidenced by the many forms of limited war which had occurred since 1945. Therefore, Taylor argued, the United States was much more likely to become involved in a conventional rather than a nuclear war.

Accordingly Taylor urged the lawmakers to take another look at the New Look and to adopt a policy of measured rather than massive retaliation, a policy of flexible response. The Army Chief of Staff stated that the Eisenhower reduction of the Army to 860,000 men had left it at least 500,000 men below minimum acceptable strength and that the budget ceilings placed upon his service had resulted in his troops possessing outmoded combat equipment and too few conventional weapons. Taylor pointed out to the Congress that Soviet armies were well equipped with third generation hardware, while 70 percent of U.S. material was of World War II vintage or older. Specifically Taylor urged the legislative branch to provide additional funds to step up development of antiaircraft and antimissile missiles, to increase our air and sea lift capability, and to expand tactical air support.[37]

Burke told the Congress that the Navy needed more funds for new ship construction, for overhauling its existing ships, and for strengthening its antisubmarine defenses against the Soviet Union's 500-submarine force. The CNO argued that both the Navy and the Marines needed more men to carry out their missions. A 600,000-man Navy and 170,000 Marines were 20 percent below minimums. Specifically he urged the legislators to speed up the Polaris program and to build an additional nuclear powered aircraft carrier, five more guided missile destroyers, and four additional nuclear attack submarines.

Even the Air Force chiefs criticized the Eisenhower budgets. Although their service was the main beneficiary of the Eisenhower strategy, receiving 46 percent of the total defense budget from 1952 to 1960, Generals Twining and White asked Congress for more fighter air wings and more rapid production of B-52 bombers and ballistic missiles.[38] Their complaints about these shortcomings in massive retaliation led to special hearings by Congress on the condition of American air power.

In fiscal year 1960, the service chiefs actually put their complaints about the Eisenhower administration in writing and sent them to Senator Lyndon Johnson's Senate Preparedness Subcommittee. The chiefs' conduct before the Congress so incensed Eisenhower that he publicly accused the JCS of legalized insubordination. The President even attempted to amend the National Security Act to take away the chiefs' prerogative of informing Congress about their disagreements with the administration's defense policy. However, since he never brought any sanctions against the offending chiefs, as did his predecessor and his successor, Eisenhower was not able to get the chiefs to be team players.

Ironically, during the last year that Eisenhower was in office, the Joint Chiefs began to move in the direction of being team players. However, it was not the result of any directive from the Commander in Chief, but of the style of Eisenhower's lame duck defense secretary, Thomas Gates. Taking office in December 1959, after having served as Secretary of the Navy and deputy secretary of defense, Gates established an excellent relationship with the chiefs. Rather than waiting for JCS papers to come up to him, or rather than dealing with the chiefs only through the chairman, Gates himself met with the entire JCS several times a week. During these meetings he saw to it that the chiefs had their innings and he never allowed them to lose face with their own service people. Gates did not ask the chiefs to compromise their views and encouraged them to appeal his decisions to higher authority. These methods created great loyalty to him and put a stop to the end runs to Congress and the press leaks that had bedeviled his predecessors.

A good example of the new attitude of the JCS was the way in which the Chief of Naval Operations reacted to the dispute over strategic targeting. With the development of Polaris submarines, the Navy had finally gained its long-sought goal of a permanent place in the strategic arena. In early 1960, Navy leaders asked the defense secretary to allow them to select their own targets for the submarine-launched ballistic missiles. After a month-long personal study of the situation, Gates turned down the Navy's request. He concluded that the targets selected for the Polaris missiles had to be coordinated with those chosen by the Strategic Air Command and he set up a unified strategic planning group under the control of the Air Force general who headed SAC. Gates' decision met with vehement opposition from CNO Arleigh Burke and the other members of the naval hierarchy. The Naval Officers Corps feared that placing Polaris under the control of an Air Force general would result in the Navy's losing control of its new weapon. The controversy appeared to have all of the elements of the "revolt of the admirals" which had occurred a decade earlier.

However, because of Gates' actions, there was not even a minor rebellion. The secretary believed that if there were strong disagreement on military policy questions, a chief should present his case to the President. Therefore, he encouraged Burke to appeal his decision directly to Eisenhower. The CNO met with the President and for five hours argued vehemently against Gates' decision. Eisenhower listened sympathetically but ruled against the Navy. Burke, upset at the decision, but grateful to the secretary for giving him the opportunity to make his case, did not revive the Organizational and Policy Research Division. Instead, he sent a message to the entire fleet. In the message Burke not only announced that he supported Gates' decision, but also ordered his subordinates to send the Navy's best people to fill the billets on the Joint Strategic Target Planning Group.[39]

Despite the publicity generated by the public statements and congressional testimony of the Joint Chiefs, there is no evidence that they affected the level of defense expenditures. Congress listened sympathetically but refused to take responsibility for significantly increasing the defense budget. And the President, who was well aware of the dangers of the military-industrial complex, invariably impounded any excess funds appropriated by the Congress. In Eisenhower's eight years in office, Congress added $2.0 billion and cut $3.8 billion for a net change of $1.8 billion, or one-half of one percent.

THE KENNEDY-JOHNSON ADMINISTRATION

Before assuming the Presidency, John Kennedy appointed a committee, headed by Senator Symington, the first Secretary of the Air Force, to study Department of Defense organization for the purpose of recommending needed changes. After two months of study, the Symington Committee proposed a radical reorganization of the department. But, when Robert McNamara accepted Kennedy's offer to become the eighth Secretary of Defense, he persuaded the young President-elect to delay proposing the reorganization until he (McNamara) could assess the situation personally. But Kennedy did give McNamara two directives: first, develop the military structure required for a firm foundation for our foreign policy without regard to budget ceilings; second, operate this force at the lowest possible cost.[40]

Armed only with those two directives, and without benefit of any new legislation, McNamara made so many changes, formal and informal, organizational and procedural, during his seven years in the Pentagon that he brought about not just a reorganization but a revolution in the Department of Defense. Nowhere was this revolution more acutely felt than in the budget process, where the eighth Secretary of Defense introduced the planning-programming-budgeting system (PPBS) and cost effectiveness (systems analysis).[41]

The PPBS divided the budgetary process into three clearly defined cycles and lengthened it to eighteen months. Thus, preparation of the fiscal year 1966 budget, which was to become effective in July 1965 and was to be submitted to the Congress in January 1965, got under way in July 1963. Cost effectiveness, or systems analysis, is a technique that looks at alternate ways of performing a job and seeks, by estimating in quantitative terms where possible, to identify the most effective alternative.

The foundation for the planning-programming-budgeting system in the defense department from 1961 through 1968 was the Five-Year Defense Plan (FYDP). This document was the master plan for the budget process and contained the programs approved by the defense office with their estimated costs projected for five years. The initial Five-Year Plan was produced in 1961 and projected programs and costs through 1965. Each year the plan was updated by decisions made during the budget process.

The planning cycle was the first and longest. It began in July and lasted until February and was composed of three steps. The first step involved production of Volume I of the Joint Strategic Operations Plan by the JCS. This volume was an assessment of the military threat facing the United States and of our national commitments projected for five years. For about five years, the JCS devoted a great deal of time and energy to producing this part of the JSOP. Since there was no Basic National Security Policy, the chiefs hoped that their estimates would furnish the basis for all subsequent budgetary decisions. They hoped to make the Joint Plan a substitute for the Basic Policy. However, by 1965 the JCS realized that the JSOP had little impact on subsequent budget decisions. In fact, they wondered if anyone even read it. Thus they began to spend less and less time on it and by 1967 had turned the job over to their subordinates.

While the JCS was working on the first part of the Joint Strategic Operations Plan, McNamara often assigned special projects to the chiefs. These projects consisted of a set of specific questions, had very short deadlines, and had great potential implications for the budget. For example, in March 1961, McNamara asked the chiefs to estimate how many bombers the United States would need in the next decade and he set a deadline of six weeks for the study.[42] The Joint Chiefs complained a great deal about these short deadlines, but always completed the studies on time. The Office of the Secretary of Defense usually found the studies lacking in many respects.[43] From 1961 through 1965, the defense office usually was content with pointing out the inconsistencies in these studies. But from 1965 onward, when the position of Assistant Secretary of Defense, Systems Analysis (SA), was established within the defense office, the Office of Systems Analysis began to make recommendations of its own and these were usually accepted by the defense secretary.

The second step of the planning cycle consisted of the submission of force level recommendations by the services and unified commands to the JCS. These recommendations were based upon the threat and commitments outlined in Volume I of the Joint Strategic Operations Plan. The third and final step of the planning cycle involved the completion of two major documents. The JCS completed Volume II of the JSOP. This part recommended the optimum force levels necessary to meet our national needs. Although the force levels were supposed to be based on the advice both of the services and of the unified commanders, the JCS rarely paid attention to the latter's ideas, and Volume II was based primarily upon service inputs. The Joint Chiefs ignored the unified commanders' requests because they were unrealistic and because the chiefs were wary of losing any power to these men, who were theoretically their equals.[44]

While the JCS was completing the Joint Strategic Operations Plan, the Office of the Secretary of Defense produced a major program memorandum (MPM) for each of the ten mission areas and support activities of the defense budget. These memoranda summarized the defense office position on the major force levels, the rationale for choices among alternatives, and the recommended force levels and funding. Although the memoranda were programming documents based upon the planning in the JSOP, their authors in fact ignored the JSOP and the major programming memoranda became both planning and programming documents, the central action instruments of the defense budget process.[45]

The programming cycle began with the defense secretary's receipt of the Joint Strategic Operations Plan and the major programming memoranda. This cycle lasted about six months (through the end of August). McNamara normally reviewed these documents for about thirty days and then provided guidance to the services for preparing program change requests (PCR), suggested modifications to the Five-Year Defense Plan. The primary factor shaping this guidance was the programming memoranda. The services normally submitted about three hundred program change requests annually to the Office of Systems Analysis, whose decisions were nearly always negative. The rejection of the change requests was attributable to three factors: the services used poor analytical techniques, their requests did not convey any sense of priority in relation to the base program, and the requested changes involved greater costs.[46]

Theoretically all program decisions should have been made before budgeting began, but this was not the case. Many of the program decisions were negotiated during and after the budgetary cycle.[47] A defense office official reported that in fiscal years 1968 and 1969, 90 percent of the final program decision documents were not written until after December 28, that is, after the conclusion of the budgetary cycle.[48]

While Systems Analysis was reviewing the program change requests, the JCS was reviewing the major programming memoranda. The chiefs' comments on the memoranda were sent to the defense secretary in July. For the remainder of the summer, McNamara and the JCS met about fifteen times to discuss the chiefs' adverse comments. From 1961 through 1965, the JCS was never united on the major issues raised in the programming memoranda. The Navy objected to the B-70; the Army opposed a fifteen-carrier fleet; and the Air Force was less than enthusiastic about the antiballistic missile. In their meetings, McNamara was able to capitalize on these differences and skillfully played one service off against another. However, from 1966 onward, the JCS worked out their differences prior to meeting with the defense secretary and presented a united front to him. For example, the Air Force wanted thirty-five wings of tactical aircraft and the Navy wanted seventeen attack carriers. Prior to meeting McNamara, they agreed on twenty-nine wings and fifteen carriers. Similar negotiations were conducted on the ABM.[49]

The chiefs realized early that McNamara was dividing and conquering but were not able to work out their differences until Taylor stepped down as chairman and Lemay was pushed out as Air

Force Chief of Staff. Taylor was regarded as an administration man and Lemay was an uncompromising crusader for air power. General Wheeler, Taylor's successor as chairman, refused to bring split opinions to McNamara. He would tell the other chiefs that he would wait until they came to some agreement before adjourning their meetings.[50] This united front eventually paid dividends for the Joint Chiefs. When they were divided McNamara could carry the day by pointing out the division to the President and Congress. But even McNamara was hesitant about overruling a united or common professional military opinion. Consequently, such items as a nuclear carrier and the ABM, which the secretary opposed for about five years, were eventually approved.

The budgetary cycle officially began in September when the services were asked to prepare their budgets in the traditional categories, that is, each service separately rather than in program packages, for submission to the Office of the Secretary of Defense by October 1. In issuing his call for budget submissions, McNamara emphatically pointed out, year after year, that the services were not to feel bound by any budgetary ceiling, real or imagined. They were to be guided only by decisions made in regard to the major programming memoranda and the program change requests. The secretary repeatedly stated that this country could afford whatever was necessary for defense.[51] Theoretically, the budgetary cycle was to consist only of costing out approved programs.

Despite McNamara's rhetoric, the JCS had a very good idea of what the total and individual service budgets would be. Sometimes the comptroller let the service chiefs know as early as July. On most occasions, it was a simple matter of arithmetic. It was more than a mere coincidence that what this country could afford for defense from fiscal year 1963 through fiscal year 1966, (before the Vietnam buildup) came within 1 percent of $46 billion each year and that the Army, Navy, and Air Force shares of the budget remained the same as under Eisenhower, a fairly constant 27, 32, and 41 percent respectively.[52] A service chief who served under

Eisenhower and McNamara said that in regard to budget ceilings there was no real difference between either administration. Another chief remarked, "Weapon systems became more and more difficult to justify as we approached our portion of $46 billion."

Any lingering doubts about a budget ceiling in the Department of Defense were shattered during the Vietnam buildup when Mc-Namara directed the services to delete programs that were not urgent, to assume for budgetary purposes that the war would be over by the end of the fiscal year and that during the year there would be no increase in the level of our commitment to Vietnam, and to stretch out maintenance and repair cycles by about 50 percent.[53] These directives made it necessary to have four consecutive supplemental budgets from 1966 through 1969, caused the Joint Chiefs to contemplate resigning en masse, destroyed McNamara's credibility with Johnson, and eventually contributed to the firing of McNamara.[54]

From 1961 through 1965, the service budget requests exceeded by about 10 percent the amount eventually approved. However, from 1966 through 1968, as McNamara's standing within the administration waned, the gap between the amount requested and the amount granted widened enormously. According to defense department figures, the requests for fiscal year 1967 exceeded by 19 percent the amount granted, and the difference climbed to 28 percent in 1968 and to over 30 percent in 1969.

From October through December, the comptroller's office reviewed these budgets. In its review, the office normally initiated some six hundred subject issues, that is, areas of potential savings. Although these issues were theoretically technical (for example, the cost of a submarine or the cost of equipping an infantry battalion), in fact the issues reflected intuitive feelings on the part of the personnel in the comptroller's office about where they felt cuts ought to be made.[55] McNamara reviewed the budgets personally and, with the subject issues as a guide, made about seven hundred budgetary decisions annually. Often his decisions concerned the smallest matters, for example, the color of belt buckles. During his review, McNamara consulted with the JCS about twenty times. These consultations took place on the secretary's terms. McNamara never allowed the chiefs to review the budget as a whole but only asked them to comment on items individually. He was not interested in whether the chiefs preferred x or y, only their opinion of x. In deliberating about x, the chiefs never knew if he would ask about y.[56]

The executive phase of the budgetary cycle concluded in late December when the President met with the defense secretary and the Joint Chiefs for about four hours. Despite vigorous opposition on the part of many members of the JCS during their "days in court," the President invariably sided with McNamara. Some of the issues raised in these meetings included the B-70, the number of Polaris submarines, and pilot shortages.

McNamara expected the Joint Chiefs of Staff to be more than military advisors. He wanted them to incorporate economic criteria into their traditional military requirement studies. Advice based on purely military judgment was useless in his eyes. The defense secretary viewed the JCS as one of the many resources available to him to be used on his terms; the chiefs were no more or no less important than any of his other advisors. The ability of the chiefs to influence policy was dependent upon the quality of their advice, not upon their position as the principal military advisors to the Secretary of Defense. McNamara expected the JCS to be satisfied with the increased level of defense spending and to accept his innovations as "more rational" than previous methods. Once he had reached a decision, the secretary expected the chiefs to support it, even if they opposed the rationale for the decision.[57]

McNamara's methods, particularly in the executive phase of the budget process, infuriated not only the JCS but nearly the entire officers corps as well. In the eyes of most of the professional military men, the planning-programming-budgeting system and systems analysis were essentially devices for substituting social science techniques for military experience and transferring the making of strategy from the military to inexperienced civilians. General Thomas White, Air Force Chief of Staff from 1957 to 1961, clearly reflected the deep resentment of the military when he stated that he was profoundly apprehensive of these so-called professional defense intellectuals. White did not believe that these arrogant young men had sufficient worldliness or motivation to stand up to the enemy.[58]

His successor as Air Force Chief of Staff, Curtis Lemay, echoed these sentiments when he complained that the military profession had been overrun by civilian pundits who set themselves up as popular oracles of military strategy. In Lemay's view, these civilian experts, without military experience, propose military strategies based upon hopes and fears rather than seasoned judgments, and these unprofessional strategists go unchallenged only because McNamara had effectively prohibited the professional active duty officers from entering the debate.[59]

Admiral Hyman Rickover, the father of the Navy's nuclear power program, compared McNamara and his civilian experts to spiritualists who tried to play God while neglecting the responsibility of being human. Testifying before Congress in May 1968, Rickover claimed that these civilians had no scientific training or technical expertise and knew little about military operations. He argued that this country was unwise to put its fate into the inexperienced hands of McNamara and his men.[60]

After being fired as CNO, George Anderson summed up the frustrations of the military men who had to work with the Secretary of Defense and his civilian associates. In a speech to the National Press Club in September 1963, Anderson stated that military men feel emotionally aroused when the recommendations of the uniformed chiefs, each backed up by competent professional staffs, are altered or overruled without interim consultation, explanation, and discussion. In Anderson's view, McNamara's analysts were working at the wrong echelon: they were operating above the professional military level rather than in an advisory capacity. These specialists were endangering national security by injecting their judgments into fields in which they had no expert knowledge.[61] It was not much of an exaggeration to say that military men under McNamara felt that they had been reduced to second-class citizens in the defense budget process. Their views appeared to be at the mercy of almost any civilian official in the Office of the Secretary of Defense.

The military was not any happier about McNamara's legislative guidelines. The secretary was quite explicit about how the Joint Chiefs should act during their congressional testimony. In a memorandum from his office, the chiefs were directed not to reveal their differences with him unless pressed by Congress, and if they did, they were also to present the secretary's position.[62] To insure conformity with this directive, someone from McNamara's office was always present when a chief was testifying.

Initially McNamara had a great deal of difficulty in getting the chiefs to follow the "party line" before Congress. Lemnitzer, Lemay, and Anderson took exception to McNamara's strategy and methods in the period from 1961 to 1963. In order to secure compliance from the chiefs, McNamara had all three of the offenders removed from the JCS and put less well known men in their place. From 1964 through 1966, McNamara's band of chiefs harmonized beautifully before the Congress. Not even the barbed questions of several members of the Armed Services and Appropriations committees could draw the chiefs into criticizing McNamara's policies or methods. So ebullient were the chiefs in their praise of the defense budgets that on several occasions some congressmen asked them if they had lost their nerve, while others accused the chiefs of letting their services down.[63]

However, by mid-1966 it became apparent to the Joint Chiefs that McNamara's dovishness was eroding his relationship with Johnson and consequently his power to retaliate against them. Therefore, in McNamara's last years in office, the chiefs openly criticized their boss and his methods before the Congress. In the spring of 1967, Chairman Wheeler read a prepared statement criticizing McNamara's position on the ABM. Admiral McDonald contended that McNamara's program deferrals were ruining his fleet, and General McConnell urged Congress to overrule the secretary's opposition to a new manned bomber to replace the aging B-52.[64] Unfortunately for the JCS, the pleas fell on deaf ears. By the end of the McNamara years, a war-weary public was starting to become tired of large defense budgets and Congress was beginning to sense this change in the land.[65]

THE FIRST NIXON
ADMINISTRATION

Melvin Laird, who had observed McNamara's revolution from his seat on the House Subcommittee on Military Appropriations, agreed with many military men that McNamara's methods had led to overcentralization in decision making and an insufficient role for the professional soldier. Accordingly, when he became the tenth Secretary of Defense, Laird instituted certain changes in the defense budget process to redress this situation. He referred to his method as participatory management. The essence of these changes was contained in a "treaty" signed by the deputy secretary of defense, the service secretaries, and the chairman of the JCS. This treaty, "negotiated" soon after Laird assumed the helm at the Pentagon, provided that the Secretary of Defense would look to the services and the JCS in the design of forces and that the Office of Systems Analysis would limit itself to evaluation and review and not put forward independent proposals of its own. In return for this concession, the secretary expected the services to operate within rigid budget ceilings.[66] As a means of emphasizing the reduced role of Systems Analysis, Laird left the post of assistant secretary for Systems Analysis vacant for a year. Eventually the head of Systems Analysis was downgraded from an assistant secretary to a director.

The defense budget was still a product of the planning-programming-budgeting system, but, as the treaty indicated, the emphasis with the process was shifted. Moreover, during the first years of the Nixon administration, the National Security Council was revitalized and the military was provided with its clearest conception of United States policy in many years. During the first three years of the Nixon administration, about 150 national security study memoranda (NSSM) were produced by the National Security Council, and many of these provided guidance for the military budget planners. In the first month of the new administration, the security study memoranda concerned such budget-related topics as military posture, American military forces, and contingency planning. NSSM 3 of January 21, 1969, resulted in a study of the tasks which American military forces should be prepared to undertake and concluded that the United States must be prepared to fight one large war and one brushfire war (one and a half wars) simultaneously rather than the somewhat impractical two and a half wars of the McNamara period.[67]

As indicated in figure 3, the planning process began eighteen months before the budget was sent to Congress and had as its foundation the Five-Year Defense Plan.[68] The JCS inaugurated the planning cycle by producing Volume I of the Joint Strategic Operations Plan (the strategic assessment) and sending it to Laird. The secretary reviewed the JSOP for conformity with National Security Council doctrine and then issued a coordinated, complete, and current strategic guidance document for the entire defense community. This strategic guidance memorandum (SGM) was essentially the JSOP with some updating and enlargement and was issued in January (for example, the memorandum for fiscal year 1972 was issued in January 1970).

In January, the secretary also issued a tentative fiscal guidance memorandum (TFGM) projecting dollar constraints for the next

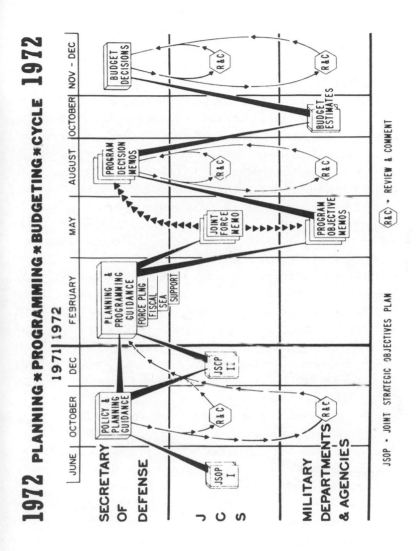

Figure 3: 1972 Planning-Programming-Budgeting-Cycle 1972

five years. While the elements of the Department of Defense were reviewing this memorandum, the JCS completed the force structure portion (Volume II) of the JSOP. This was prepared from a purely military perspective, without regard to the fiscal constraints of the tentative fiscal guidance memorandum. The defense secretary reviewed the comments on the tentative memorandum and Volume II of the JSOP and then completed the planning cycle by issuing a fiscal guidance memorandum (FGM) in March. This document set definite ceilings on the total budget and on each service. During the first Nixon administration the overall ceiling ranged from $75 to $70 billion, divided almost evenly among the services.[69]

The overall ceiling for the fiscal guidance memorandum was negotiated between Laird and the Defense Program Review Committee (DPRC), a subcommittee within the National Security Council system composed of the President's assistant for national security affairs, the deputy secretary of defense, the undersecretary of state, the chairman of the JCS, the director of the Office of Management and Budget, and the chairman of the President's Council of Economic Advisers. The task of this committee is to anticipate the political, economic, and social implications resulting from changes in defense spending, budgeting, and force levels. This body was created in October 1969, and has provided inputs for all of the budgets since fiscal year 1971.[70]

The programming cycle began in April when the JCS drew up a joint force memorandum (JFM), which presented the chiefs' recommendations on force levels and support programs that could be provided within the fiscal constraints of the fiscal guidance memorandum. The joint force document also included an assessment of the risks in these forces as measured against the strategy and objectives of the Joint Strategic Operations Plan, Volume I, and a comparison of the costs of its recommendations with the Five-Year Defense Plan. Finally, the joint force memorandum highlighted the major force issues to be resolved during the year. In May, each service submitted to the Secretary of Defense a program objective memorandum (POM) for each major mission area and support activity in the defense budget. These memoranda expressed total program requirements in terms of forces, manpower, and costs and provided a rationale for deviations from the Five-Year Plan and the joint force memorandum. The Office of the Secretary of Defense no longer issued program documents, but confined itself to reviewing those submitted by the JCS and the services. In July Laird completed the programming cycle by issuing program decision memoranda (PDM) for each budget area. These memoranda were a product of the Joint Strategic Operations Plan, the joint force memorandum, the program objective memoranda, and the analysis of these documents performed in the secretary's office by his systems analysts. The Five-Year Defense Plan was updated each summer by these program decision memoranda.

During the rest of the year, the defense secretary met with the JCS to resolve any disputes over the program decision memoranda. Laird was desirous of achieving consensus with the chiefs and these meetings developed into real negotiating and bargaining sessions and resulted in compromises between the parties. For example, the secretary allowed the Air Force to build two prototypes of the B-1 before committing the department to full production. Likewise, Laird got the Navy to drop its demand for a nuclear carrier in fiscal year 1972 by promising to support the carrier in the 1973 and 1974 budgets. Moreover, when Laird had to turn down a JCS request for monetary reasons or because of a decision made by the administration, he encouraged the chiefs to take their case to other agencies within the executive branch, for example, the Office of Management and Budget, the Treasury, the Defense Program Review Committee, or even the Oval Office. The only restriction placed on this practice was that a service chief must make his case on its own merits and not at the expense of another service. Finally, if the Joint Chiefs were able to convince Laird that their position had more merit than administration policy, the secretary would join them in trying to win a reversal of the decision. For example, when the JCS objected to the new military retirement plan pro-posed by an administration study, Laird appointed a group within the Pentagon to study the administration's plan and stymied all action on the proposal. Likewise, in fiscal year 1972, when the JCS convinced him that there would be too many weaknesses in the military force that could be produced within the administration's $70 billion ceiling, Laird succeeded in convincing the President to allocate an additional $6 billion to defense.[71]

The budgetary cycle commenced on September 30, when each service submitted its budget to the Secretary of Defense. The bud-gets were supposed to be based on the approved programs resulting from the various decision documents produced in the program cycle. In each year that Laird was in office, these budget requests were within 5 percent of the established ceilings. The estimates were reviewed during October and November by the defense office staff and representatives of the Office of Management and Budget. From fiscal year 1970 to fiscal year 1973, these officials reduced these submissions by an average of 3.7 percent, far less than had previous administrations and even Congress.[72]

Before going to the President, the defense budget was reviewed by the Defense Program Review Committee. However, because of the time constraints, the impact of this body has been minimal. In the week or so that the committee has to review the budget, it could hardly be expected to make major changes. In 1970 and 1971, the committee tried to become involved earlier in the budget cycle by reviewing Laird's strategic guidance memorandum and setting fiscal constraints on certain areas, but the secretary successfully resisted these efforts to encroach upon his perceived area of bureaucratic responsibility. By the end of Nixon's first administration, the chair-man of the Defense Program Review Committee had become so in-volved with other problems, such as the Strategic Arms Limitation Talks and the Middle East, that the committee dropped its attempt to reshape the defense budget. Its main impact has been in the area of overall fiscal guidance.

Nixon allowed the JCS to have their day in court usually in late December or early January. Each chief was allowed about fifteen minutes to brief the President, although sometimes a more exuberant chief, like Zumwalt, might take more time. These sessions did not result in any major changes in the budget under review, but did serve to strengthen the President's resolve to fight for certain programs before the Congress and to lay the foundation for the upcoming budget.

Since 1969, the JCS has been facing a Congress that is becoming increasingly disenchanted with defense programs. Congressional reductions in the first Nixon administration amounted to an average of 5.3 percent or $4 billion annually. The chiefs were so overwhelmed trying to justify their portion of the administration budget that they had no chance to ask for increments or to criticize the policies of the administration or the programs of the other services. Moreover, they realized that any attempt to do so would only weaken their own position. The Nixon chiefs were fairly successful on the hill. Although congressional reductions were large in fiscal terms, Congress did not affect any of the key JCS programs, for example, the B-1, the Trident, the F-14, the S-3A, and the F-15.[73]

Laird had a very clear conception of the role that the Joint Chiefs should play in the budget process. Within broad guidelines established by his office, he expected them to take the initiative in the development of programs, subject to a final review by his office. He wanted them to work within clearly established budget ceilings and, through a process of negotiation and bargaining with him, to take responsibility for the forces developed within those ceilings. The defense secretary did not want to see an outbreak of the interservice rivalry that followed each previous war when defense budgets were reduced in real terms.

The JCS apparently lived up to Laird's expectations and their relationship was quite harmonious. Their requested budgets were always close to the established ceilings and there were no public outbreaks of interservice rivalries. For example, in the vigorous debate within Congress over the Trident, Admiral Zumwalt did not make his case at the expense of the Air Force's B-1. The CNO's argument was based on Russian activities, not those of another service. The Laird chiefs apparently realized that they had to be "team players." Without support in Congress or from the public, their only source of strength lay in an administration and a secretary committed to a strong national defense posture.

CONCLUSION

Perhaps the best way to begin to summarize this analysis of the role of the JCS in the defense budget process would be to identify the essential elements in the executive phase of that process. The preceeding sections indicated that, despite changes in style or emphasis from secretary to secretary, there are four steps which are common to all post–World War II administrations: They are (1) the establishment of the overall size of the military budget; (2) the production of strategic plans to guide the distribution of defense funds; (3) the preparation and submission of departmental budget requests; and (4) review and revision of these requests.

The JCS has had virtually no impact upon determining the actual size of the military budget. All of the administrations have arrived at a figure for defense based upon factors quite apart from the opinions of the Joint Chiefs and often times have resisted strenuous efforts on the part of the chiefs to raise the ceilings. The first two postwar administrations relied on magic number ceilings. President Truman decided that one-third of the budget would go for defense purposes, while his Republican successor decided that no more than 10 percent of the gross national product could be allotted to the military. Neither Kennedy nor Johnson had recourse to any magic numbers, but they imposed specific constraints on McNamara before he made his allegedly open-ended program decisions. This was especially evident during Vietnam, when Johnson was striving for both "guns and butter" and placed unrealistic constraints upon a wartime budget. The Nixon administration's ceilings were based on the gross national product, the anticipated reaction of Congress, and the desire to have a balanced full employment budget.

For the past twenty-five years, the JCS has developed strategic plans to guide the distribution of defense funds. These master plans have been referred to as the JSOP (Joint Strategic Operations Plan) for most of the period. In the Truman, Eisenhower, and Nixon administrations, these plans were related to guidelines developed by the National Security Council, while, in the McNamara years, the JSOP was written without any advice from the civilian leaders. Despite the time and effort spent on the JSOP, there is no evidence that it has any real impact upon defense budgeting. As a matter of fact, it has been totally irrelevant and often goes unread by the key officials. The Joint Chiefs were not the only ones developing unrealistic budget plans over the past twenty-five years. The National Security Council plans of the Truman administration, the Basic National Security Policy of the Eisenhower era, McNamara's major program memoranda, and Laird's strategic guidance memoranda have also been of little use in the budget process.

The main beneficiaries of this gap between planning and budgeting have been the service chiefs. With no operative framework, the Joint Chiefs have been free to request nearly anything they want in the third essential step, the preparation and submission of the monetary requests. Because of the absence of any real link between the plans and the budgets, such factors as program decisions and administration priorities have not affected the things requested by the chiefs to any great degree.

However, the chiefs are almost without influence in the final step of the process, the budgeting review. Ironically, during the Truman and Eisenhower administrations they could have dominated the review, but they were not ready to accept the responsibility. However, when they tried to establish priorities during

McNamara's reviews, the secretary refused to allow them to do so. Under Laird the reviews have not been very significant because the services requests have been very close to the ceilings.

Although there have been brief periods during the Truman and Eisenhower administrations and the McNamara years when the chiefs have allowed themselves to be pressured into tacitly supporting defense policies with which they disagreed, the JCS has generally played a very active role in the legislative phase of budgetary process. The Truman administration witnessed the "revolt of the admirals"; the Eisenhower chiefs sent a written statement to Lyndon Johnson; Chairman Earl Wheeler read a prepared pro-ABM and anti-McNamara statement to the Congress; and the Nixon chiefs vigorously defended many controversial weapon systems on Capitol Hill. However, the JCS has had little impact upon the Congress. Despite the publicity often generated during the legislative phase, the Congress has shown itself unwilling to make real program choices in the defense budget.

Except for the Nixon administration, the Joint Chiefs have consistently disappointed the expectations of their civilian superiors. Truman and Eisenhower wanted the JCS to work within and publicly support ceilings developed primarily on political and economic grounds, while McNamara demanded that the JCS use and extol a methodology, which placed very little importance on military experience, for deciding the size and distribution of the defense budget. Except on a few occasions, the JCS refused to share responsibility for the ceilings or the methodology before the Congress, the American people, or their service subordinates.

In the first Nixon administration, the JCS played exactly the role that the administration had envisioned for it. David Packard, Laird's deputy secretary of defense, called the Joint Chiefs the finest, most dedicated, most capable men he had ever known and stated that they had given Secretary Laird their complete support and cooperation.[74] The reasons for the JCS switch in modus operandi are many, but perhaps the most important is the changed attitude of the American people toward defense spending. If the chiefs do not take responsibility for the administration's budget before the Congress and the people, they will no longer get a sympathetic hearing. Before 1969, the military leaders could always find a sympathetic constituency that would support their claims against the administration, but now their only real supporters are in the administration.

In evaluating the role of the JCS in the budget process, it is not sufficient to consider only whether the chiefs have fulfilled the expectations of our elected officials. There is an issue that is more important for the well-being of the American political system: did the Joint Chiefs of Staff dominate the process to such an extent that this nation spent more on defense than its elected leaders desired? Or, were they denied sufficient input into the process with the result that our civilian leaders made their budgetary decisions without the benefit of expert military opinion?

This analysis has shown that the answer to both of these questions must be negative. The JCS had very little impact upon the size of the defense budget. The starting point for the bottom line was not JCS plans but real political and economic constraints. Moreover, while some civilian officials turned a deaf ear to JCS advice, the chiefs were eventually able to make their positions known within the administration and to the Congress. Let us now see if the wartime activities of the JCS present as balanced a picture.

★

CHAPTER FOUR

The
Operational Role

Nothing brings the JCS into public view more forcefully than the outbreak of war. Yet, as was noted in the first chapter, the Joint Chiefs have very little authority in the operational realm. The chiefs do not have any forces under their control and are excluded from the chain of command. The chain presently goes from the President through the Secretary of Defense to one of the unified commanders. The chiefs are merely advisers to the President and the defense secretary in the exercise of their command authority, and there is no legal requirement for these civilian leaders to consult the Joint Chiefs or even keep them informed of their decisions on operational matters.[1] Nevertheless, every time an armed conflict arises, the Joint Chiefs seem to be involved and are usually held responsible for the consequences of operational decisions. For example, in February 1968, Lyndon Johnson demanded that the JCS sign a statement which indicated that it was their expert opinion that the beleaguered outpost at Khe Sanh could be held against North Vietnamese assaults. The President made the chiefs do this even though they were 7,000 miles from the scene and had no say in establishing the outposts or providing for their defense. These decisions were made by the field commander, General Westmoreland.

There is no doubt that the JCS does play a role in the operational area. Every government study of the Department of Defense from the first Hoover Commission to the Fitzhugh Panel has recommended that the chiefs divorce themselves from the operational realm and operate primarily as a planning agency. Yet, none of the studies has ever addressed the related questions of how and why the JCS does become involved, what that involvement consists of, or what the impact of the JCS is on operational matters.

In the twenty-five years since the creation of the Department of Defense, the cold war has turned very hot for the United States on two occasions, Korea (1950–53) and Vietnam (1964–73). In addition to these two shooting wars, each of which involved the commitment of several hundred thousand American fighting men, the United States has been confronted with several crises which have resulted in the use of small numbers of American troops or the threat of military action: Berlin, the Congo, Laos, the Middle East, Cuba, and the Dominican Republic. A detailed analysis of JCS activities in every crisis would result in several books. This chapter will begin by summarizing the role of the chiefs in these crisis situations and then move on to a detailed discussion of the part that the JCS played in the two shooting wars in which the United States has become engaged. These two wars involved each of the postwar administrations and encompassed all of the reorganizations that affected the chiefs' operational authority .

In the crisis situations of the post–World War II period which did not evolve into armed conflicts, the Joint Chiefs of Staff played a minor role. During some of these situations the chiefs were not even consulted. For example, the JCS was not involved in the initial decision to commit four hundred troops to the Dominican Republic in 1965. This critical decision was taken at a White House meeting on April 28, 1965, at which the Secretary of Defense, the Secretary of State, the director of Central Intelligence, the United Nations ambassador, the presidential assistant for national security affairs, eight senators, and six congressmen were present, but to which no member of the JCS was invited.[2] On other occasions, the Joint Chiefs were consulted after the fact, primarily to legitimize decisions already made. For example, during the Cuban missile crisis, President Kennedy met with the JCS after he had tentatively decided on a blockade, and he became annoyed with the chiefs because they would not endorse his decision. The JCS preferred a more violent response, either an air strike or an invasion.[3] In the Bay of Pigs episode of 1961, the Joint Chiefs were asked to give their opinion of a plan which had been developed and would be implemented by the CIA. The chiefs were not the authors of the plan and only discovered the existence of the operation by accident. Moreover, their approval was less than enthusiastic and was based on the mistaken impression that the operation had already been ratified by President Kennedy.[4]

When they have been consulted before decisions have been made, the chiefs usually have been very cautious about using military force. The JCS recommended noninvolvement in the Hungarian revolt of 1956, the Suez Canal campaign of that same year, and the Congo crisis of 1960. In addition, the JCS opposed any steps to tear down the Berlin Wall in 1961 or the commitment of troops to Laos in 1962. The JCS also opposed retaliating against North Korea after the Communist nation captured the *Pueblo* in 1964 and shot down an EC-121 aircraft in 1969. The chiefs also were opposed to intervening in the Middle East to save the government of Lebanon in 1958 or that of Jordan in 1970.[5]

However, when the President has resorted to armed intervention, the chiefs have generally supported the quick application of overwhelming force. During the debates over intervention in Indo-China in 1954 and Laos in 1961, the JCS supported the involvement of American troops only on condition that the troops be given permission to employ nuclear weapons if necessary. Likewise, in the Dominican crisis of 1965, after the intervention decision had been made, the JCS advised the President to commit 22,000 troops and a large number of ships to prevent a Communist takeover.[6]

Let us move now to a discussion of Korea and Vietnam to see if the impact of the JCS is different once the shooting starts.

KOREA[7]

Background

Officially the Korean War lasted for just over three years, from late June 1950 until July 1953. However, most of the real decisions about conducting the war took place within the first year; one year after the outbreak of hostilities, negotiations between the United Nations forces and the Communist side had already begun. The peace conference deadlocked for two years over the issue of prisoner of war repatriation, and battlefield action was confined primarily to a "battle for hills" along a fairly static front very close to the original North-South demarcation line. It was during the first year of the war that the Truman administration was confronted with the actual attack, the debates on the nature and scope of the American response, the massive Chinese intervention, the insubordination by MacArthur, and the Russian call for peace talks. This chapter will focus on the part that the Joint Chiefs played in those five episodes that first hectic year of the Korean War.

The Attack

Soon after the passage of the National Security Act, President Truman instructed Secretary of State Marshall to request a JCS estimate of the importance of South Korea from the point of view

of the military security of the United States. The JCS recommended that the 45,000 men stationed in South Korea could be
used more profitably elsewhere and should be evacuated as soon
as possible for three reasons.[8]

First, the huge reductions in defense spending left the United
States with a skeleton military force. As noted in chapter three,
defense spending had fallen from $85 to $10 billion between
1945 and 1950. The 45,000 troops in South Korea represented
about 9 percent of the total Army strength in the fall of 1947.
Although occupation of the Korean peninsula could allow an
enemy to threaten Japan, the peninsula was not of sufficient strategic importance to the United States to justify a commitment of
9 percent of our ground troops.

Second, the JCS felt that the next war would probably be a
total war with the Soviet Union and would most likely be precipitated by an attack upon America's first line of defense in Western
Europe. Therefore, the vast majority of the limited resources of
this country should be concentrated in Europe. In a total war
with the Russians, the Korean peninsula would be of minor strategic importance at best.

Third, defending Korea presented huge logistic difficulties. It
was 5,000 miles from the United States and its terrain was unsuit-
able for the application of American military power. General
Bradley summarized the problems of a war in Korea when he
succinctly stated that the chiefs hoped that the United States would
never have to fight in Korea because it is such a poor place to
fight.[9] Accordingly, the troops were withdrawn in 1948, and over
the next two years both Secretary of State Acheson and General
MacArthur, the Far East commander, made public pronouncements
which apparently excluded South Korea from the American defense perimeter. When the North Koreans attacked on June 25,
1950, American forces in South Korea consisted of a 500-man
military advisory group.

The Decision to Become Involved

Despite the fact that they too had excluded Korea from the American defense perimeter, the Joint Chiefs eventually joined Truman's other advisors in supporting the decision to intervene militarily on the Korean peninsula. However, the recommendation to intervene originated with the Secretary of State, not with the JCS or even the Department of Defense. As Secretary of Defense Louis Johnson later testified, "Neither I nor any member of the Military Establishment . . . recommended we go into Korea. The recommendation came from the Secretary of State. . . ."[10] The Joint Chiefs of Staff supported the decision to intervene, but not because they had changed their opinion about the strategic importance of Korea. Indeed, all during the deliberations, which spanned five days and five meetings with the President, the chiefs consistently argued that Korea was of no strategic value to the United States. Rather, the chiefs supported the decision to intervene because they felt that failure to respond to direct Communist aggression in Korea would whet the aggressor's appetite and would undermine the credibility of an American response to aggression in other more important locations.

According to Bradley, the JCS thought that the Soviet move in Korea was a "softening up operation" and "the first step on a timetable of aggressions, the final stage of which, if uninterrupted, would be World War III."[11] Air Force Chief Vandenberg stated the JCS "believed that somewhere, sometime we had to stop being pushed around," and that we had "to afford some hope to those people, who lined themselves up with us, that they could expect some assistance from the United States."[12]

Army Chief of Staff Collins supported the intervention on the same grounds as the other chiefs, but added an additional justification. Failure to stop the aggression in Korea would doom the United Nations to the same fate as befell the League of Nations. Collins told Congress that the United Nations "may not be effective, but, by God, until it is proven completely ineffective, I think we ought to do everything in our power to make it work."[13]

The Joint Chiefs initially disagreed over the form of the American response. On the day of the attack, Admiral Sherman and General Vandenberg advised the President that naval and air power would be sufficient. Army General Collins and General Bradley disagreed and argued that ground troops would be needed. The President initially authorized only air and naval attacks, but five days after the invasion MacArthur reported to Collins that North Korea was routing the South Koreans and that only American ground troops could save the situation; he asked for authority to send two divisions to the beleaguered area. MacArthur's recommendation was considered at a meeting at the White House on June 30 and was unanimously approved by all of Truman's civilian and military advisors, including the JCS. However, Sherman and Vandenberg approved the decision quite reluctantly. Sherman felt that the decision to commit infantry to battle was unavoidable, but that fighting Asiatics on the Asian mainland was full of hazards and that American ground units should be disengaged as soon as it became feasible.[14]

At this same meeting, the President and his advisors discussed Chiang Kai-shek's offer to send 33,000 troops to Korea. The President was inclined to accept the Generalissimo's offer but was opposed by Acheson and the JCS. The Secretary of State felt that introducing Chinese Nationalist forces would bring in the Chinese Communists. The Joint Chiefs argued that Chiang's forces were not likely to be of much help against Soviet armor and that American transportation facilities could be better used for our own troops and supplies. The President was persuaded by these arguments and reluctantly declined Chiang's offer.[15]

Prior to announcing his decision to commit American ground

troops, President Truman met with about thirty congressmen to inform them of his decision. At this meeting, Senator Alexander Smith (R-N.J.) suggested that the President seek a congressional resolution approving this action. On July 3, 1950, the President assembled a group of fourteen people, including Bradley, at Blair House to discuss Smith's suggestion. General Bradley was one of the leaders of the group opposed to accepting Smith's suggestion. He stated that the majority in Congress were satisfied and that the irreconcilable minority might delay and debate the resolution so that its effect would be diluted.[16] Bradley's view prevailed and, partially as a result of the efforts of the Chairman of the JCS, the nation, without backing from its legislative branch, embarked upon a war that would result in over 30,000 American deaths.

The Scope of the Involvement: Inchon, The 38th Parallel, and the Chinese Intervention

Despite the fact that the Joint Chiefs unanimously supported the involvement of American ground troops in Korea, they wanted to avoid becoming too deeply involved in that Asian peninsula. Although the North Korean attack had loosened the budgetary restrictions, it would take time to build up American strength to what the chiefs considered an acceptable level. For the JCS, Europe was still the area of most importance, and while they wanted to repel the North Korean invasion, they were not sure to what extent they were willing to go to insure that objective. The field commander, General MacArthur, suffered from no such indecision, and within two weeks after the invasion, MacArthur was forcing the JCS to take a definite stand on the way in which the war would be conducted.

On July 7, MacArthur informed the JCS that he planned to defeat the North Koreans by means of an amphibious strike deep behind their lines at Inchon, a west coast post near Seoul. Two weeks later, the general cabled the JCS that he planned to land two divisions at Inchon on September 15, 1950. MacArthur favored an amphibious operation over a frontal assault because the latter would involve higher casualties. He selected Inchon because of its proximity to the capital and because the poor landing conditions there made it an unlikely target. In preparation for "Operation Chromite," as the landing would be called, MacArthur asked the JCS to send him at least eight divisions and all component services, including an airborne regimental combat team and an armored group of four medium tank battalions. Dispatching these 250,000 troops to Korea would leave only the 82nd Airborne Division as the entire general reserve in the United States.

Initially, the JCS vigorously opposed MacArthur's plan, for two reasons. First, the poor landing conditions at Inchon made an amphibious operation there extremely risky, about a 5,000-to-1 shot, in their estimation.[17] Second, the operation would require the commitment of so many forces so quickly that the strategic reserve in the United States would be practically stripped bare, Japan would be left undefended, and the Pusan perimeter, our last foothold in Korea, would be seriously jeopardized.

Although the Joint Chiefs were strongly opposed to Operation Chromite, they were reluctant to challenge MacArthur directly, for four reasons. First, as a rule, military staff officers are reluctant to overrule the on-scene commander from a distance of thousands of miles. Second, the JCS on the whole had had little experience in Asia. Only Sherman had spent a significant part of World War II in the Pacific Theatre. Third, MacArthur was senior to the JCS, both in age and in rank. The Far East Commander was seventy years old, while Chairman Bradley was only fifty-five. MacArthur was the superintendent of the academy when Vandenberg was a cadet. Moreover, MacArthur was a five-star general, while the chiefs had only four stars.[18] Fifth, and probably most important, there was MacArthur's personality and his prior relationships with the Pentagon hierarchy.

MacArthur's personality and his strained relationships with the Pentagon hierarchy became crucial variables in determining the attitude of the JCS toward him during his tenure as the operational commander.[19] The general was not just another field commander. He was a legend in his own time, a prominent national figure in the United States since he strode through the trenches in World War I armed only with a riding crop. After serving as superintendent of the military academy and as Chief of Staff under Franklin Roosevelt, he retired to the Philippines only to be called out of retirement to assume command of the desperate battle against the Japanese. MacArthur not only waged a successful campaign, but again captured the public's imagination with his dramatic promise to return to the Philippines. After the war, as supreme commander of the Allied powers, he ruled Japan almost single-handedly, often defying the requests of the civilian heads of the Allied governments, including President Truman. When MacArthur was given command of the United Nations forces in Korea, the *New York Times* editors summed up the general feeling about MacArthur when they wrote: "Fate could not have chosen a man better qualified to command the unreserved confidence of the people of this country. Here is a superb strategist and an inspired leader, a man of infinite patience and quiet stability under adverse pressure; a man equally capable of bold and decisive action."[20]

Only two people in the Pentagon had anywhere near the prestige of MacArthur. They were Secretary of Defense George Marshall and Chairman of the JCS Omar Bradley. Marshall, whom President Truman called "the greatest living American," was the same age as MacArthur and, like him, a five-star general and a former Army Chief of Staff. In addition, Marshall had also held the distinguished position of Secretary of State. However, the relationship between the two five-star generals was anything but harmonious. Between the world wars, Chief of Staff MacArthur was alleged to have prevented then Colonel Marshall from be-

coming a general. But during World War II their roles were reversed. Chief of Staff Marshall was now superior to Far East
Commander MacArthur. Moreover, Marshall adopted the philos-
ophy that the war in Europe was America's first priority, much
to the dismay of MacArthur who was fighting in Asia and felt that
it deserved priority. After World War II, Marshall failed to arrange
a truce between the Nationalists and Communists in China and
was blamed by MacArthur for the beginning of the crumbling of
American power in continental Asia.

Bradley was a member of West Point's class of 1915, the
"Class of Generals." Among his famous classmates was Dwight
Eisenhower. Like Marshall and MacArthur, Bradley had served
as Army Chief of Staff, and in the fall of 1950 would also become
a five-star general. Because of Bradley's close personal and professional association with Marshall, his relations with MacArthur
suffered some of the same strains as those of the Secretary of Defense. Bradley and Marshall had served together at the infantry
school from 1929 to 1933, and Bradley had served as assistant
secretary of Marshall's general staff from 1939 to 1941. During
World War II, Bradley subscribed to Marshall's view of the priority of Europe over Asia and was a distinguished commander in
the European theater. Bradley led the 1st Army in the Normandy
invasion and, during the drive to the Rhine, commanded the 12th
Army Group, consisting of four armies and 1.3 million men, the
largest body of American soldiers ever to serve under one field
commander.

The JCS therefore had to be wary of overruling a commander
with such wide public support and prestige, and Bradley and
Marshall had to be on guard lest their opinions about MacArthur
be perceived as a continuation of their personal difficulties with
the general.

The JCS was not alone in opposing the Inchon landing. Administration officials, the Navy and Marine commanders who
would have to execute the plan, and General Walker, commander

of the 8th Army at Pusan, also opposed Operation Chromite as too risky. Two attempts were made to talk MacArthur out of the landing. In early August, Averell Harriman, the President's personal representative, and Generals Ridgway and Norstad, deputy chiefs of staff for Collins and Vandenberg, met with MacArthur, and in late August, Sherman and Collins of the JCS went to Tokyo. Despite the strenuous arguments raised by these men against Chromite, MacArthur refused to budge and eventually persuaded everyone that the operation was at least "not impossible." Admiral Sherman, the most skeptical of all the chiefs, finally approved and said, "I wish I had that man's confidence." On August 29, the Joint Chiefs of Staff formally, if somewhat reluctantly, approved the landing. Their reluctance was shown about a week before the start of the operation, when they asked MacArthur if the landing could be postponed.[21]

Operation Chromite was not postponed and succeeded beyond all expectations. But the success of the operation soon presented the administration and the JCS with new problems. Fifteen days after the Inchon landing, allied troops had cleared South Korea of Communist troops and MacArthur asked for permission to pursue the fleeing troops into North Korea. The Joint Chiefs were still wary of being drawn too deeply into Korea and feared that entrance of American forces into North Korea might provoke Soviet and Chinese intervention. The chiefs were also unwilling to overrule MacArthur so soon after the spectacular success at Inchon. Therefore, the JCS recommended to the administration that MacArthur be allowed to conduct military operations north of the 38th parallel to destroy the North Korean Army provided that he adhere to certain restrictions. First, the general had to submit all his plans to the JCS for approval. Second, operations in the North were contingent upon the nonintervention of the Russians and the Chinese. Third, MacArthur's forces could not cross the Manchurian or Soviet borders. Fourth, no non-Korean ground forces were to be used in the northern provinces, which bordered Manchuria.

Finally, air and naval action against Manchuria and the Soviet Union was not permitted.[22]

President Truman approved the JCS recommendations and MacArthur crossed the 38th parallel in late September. Within the next two weeks, two events occurred which were to strain the relationship between MacArthur and the JCS and the President and eventually lead to the dismissal of the field general.

First, at the same time that the JCS restrictions were transmitted to MacArthur, General Marshall, who had taken over as Secretary of Defense, sent a personal message to the commander. Marshall's "eyes only" telegram told MacArthur he was not to feel hampered tactically or strategically as he proceeded across the 38th parallel. Marshall sent the message as a good will gesture on his part because of his past difficulties with MacArthur. The secretary also wanted to soothe MacArthur's feelings over having to submit his plans to the JCS for approval.[23] The message was not cleared or coordinated with the Joint Chiefs, and MacArthur was later to imply that this message voided the JCS restrictions. Second, in mid-October, Truman and Bradley flew to Wake Island to confer with MacArthur. At this meeting, MacArthur assured the Commander in Chief and the chairman of the JCS that the Chinese would not enter the war. The general would later argue that his prediction was based upon the understanding that, if the Chinese did enter, the restrictions against the use of military power against China would not apply. Truman and Bradley contended that no such assurance was given to MacArthur.[24]

After being given permission to move north of the 38th parallel, MacArthur moved rapidly toward the Yalu River. The pace of the advance and the wide dispersion of allied forces alarmed the JCS. The chiefs thought that MacArthur had spread himself too thin and would be very vulnerable to an attack should the Chinese decide to make one. Moreover, it was clear to them that MacArthur was violating their directive about using American forces in the northern provinces. The JCS felt that the use of American troops near the Chinese frontier would unnecessarily provoke the Chinese. When the JCS questioned MacArthur about this use of American forces, the theater commander replied that his decision had been prompted by military necessity. Although they realized that this was setting a dangerous precedent, the chiefs did nothing. They knew MacArthur would ignore them anyway, and the only sanction against a recalcitrant commander, dismissal, was out of the question. Neither they nor the administration was ready for such a step so soon after Inchon.[25]

Throughout November, MacArthur's dispersed forces advanced rapidly toward the Yalu. On November 17, MacArthur informed the JCS that he would start a general offensive toward the Yalu, and on November 24, 1950, MacArthur flew to Korea and announced to the press that American troops would be home by Christmas. That same day the JCS "suggested" that, in order not to provoke the Chinese, MacArthur stop on the high ground commanding the Yalu River and spare the hydroelectric plants in North Korea. MacArthur brushed aside this suggestion as utterly impossible and the Joint Chiefs once again refused to give him a direct order.[26]

Four days after MacArthur's announcement of his "home by Christmas offensive," the Chinese launched a massive attack on the advancing, widely dispersed Americans and sent them reeling backward into South Korea. At the end of November, MacArthur cabled the JCS that we now had an entirely new war on our hands, and on December 3, MacArthur advised the chiefs that, unless positive and immediate action to widen the war was taken, the United Nations forces would ultimately be destroyed. This time, the Joint Chiefs did not allow themselves to be intimidated by MacArthur. They refused to give MacArthur more troops, nor would they allow him to widen the scope of the war. Moreover, they directed the general to prepare for the evacuation of Korea if necessary. It was their opinion that the Chinese were strong enough to drive our forces out of Korea if they chose to apply their full strength, but the Joint Chiefs were not willing to increase our effort there to prevent this from happening.[27] To the JCS, this was now the wrong war at the wrong time, in the wrong place, and with the wrong enemy.

However, the chiefs never had to face the situation. In early January, Collins and Vandenberg flew to Korea to assess the situation themselves. When they returned to Washington on January 17, they reported that the emergency had passed and that the United Nations forces were now ready to resume the offensive.[28] One week later these forces launched a counterattack, which lasted two months and drove the Communist forces back north of the 38th parallel. For the next two years U.N. and Communist forces took turns launching offensives and counteroffensives. Neither succeeded in moving the other side very far, and the final cease-fire line in July 1953 was nearly identical to the northern-most advance of the U.N. counterattack.

The Dismissal of MacArthur and the Downfall of the JCS

The stalemate on the battlefield proved very frustrating to Mac-Arthur. He mistakenly assumed that the military views of the Joint Chiefs of Staff coincided with his and that their directives to him were occasioned by pressure from civilian leaders. Therefore, he constantly spoke out against the immoral war of attrition and urged the administration to seek victory by carrying the war to the Chinese mainland, unilaterally if necessary. Now that Mac-Arthur's reputation for infallibility had been tarnished by the Chinese entrance into the war and their success against the widely scattered allied troops, the JCS was no longer afraid to overrule MacArthur, even on military grounds.

General Vandenberg, the Air Force Chief of Staff, stated that there were three reasons why the bombing of Manchuria would be militarily unwise. First, destruction of the cities of mainland China would be inconclusive because China's arsenals lay in the Soviet Union. Second, the attrition resulting from such an attack would leave this nation's air arms naked for several years and undermine our deterrent capability. Third, going it alone in Asia could mean going it alone in Europe and could deprive the United States of its bases in Europe and North Africa. This would require a five- to six-fold increase in the size of the Air Force.

Admiral Sherman argued that an economic blockade against China would be too limited in its effectiveness to bring pressure upon the Chinese to end the war quickly. Sherman felt that the limitations arose from two considerations. First, China was so economically undeveloped that the blockade would not have much effect. Second, the long Chinese-Russian border would make any naval blockade incomplete. Finally, both Bradley and Collins felt that China could not be defeated without a total commitment of almost all of this nation's ground troops. These Army leaders argued that committing this many troops to Korea would weaken us to the point that the Soviets might be tempted to launch a ground attack elsewhere.[29]

JCS resistance to MacArthur's proposals made it easier for the Truman administration, which was also opposed to widening the war, to turn down the field commander. The general became so frustrated by the unwillingness of the people in Washington to accept his advice that in the spring of 1951 he took a series of actions which led to his downfall. On March 24, 1951, Mac-Arthur issued a statement which threatened the Chinese with retaliation against their homeland if they did not make peace. This public pronouncement undercut an ongoing administration effort, which MacArthur had been informed of by the JCS,[30] to secure a cease-fire at the 38th parallel. In early April, MacArthur wrote a letter to House minority leader Joseph Martin (R-Mass.) agreeing with the congressman's stand on the use of Nationalist forces in Korea. When Martin made the letter public, Truman asked his advisers what should be done about MacArthur's defiance. The JCS met with Secretary Marshall and unanimously agreed that MacArthur had encroached upon the authority of the President and should be relieved of all his commands and be replaced by Lieutenant General Matthew B. Ridgway, then commander of the 8th Army in Korea.[31]

JCS relations with Ridgway and his successor, Mark Clark, were considerably different than they had been with MacArthur. Neither of these officers had the stature of their five-star predecessor, and both were in sympathy with the Joint Chiefs' limited war strategy. Moreover, for the duration of the war, the battlefront was relatively static and there were no major innovations like Operation Chromite to be considered. The real action had shifted to the peace table at Panmunjom, where the main issue revolved around the question of forcible repatriation of prisoners of war. The military operations that did take place were all coordinated with the JCS. Ridgway could hardly have ignored JCS directives, for while serving as deputy chief of staff of the Army during the early days of the Korean War, Ridgway had consistently challenged the Joint Chiefs to rein in their overzealous field commander.[32]

Although their relations with the field commanders improved, the Joint Chiefs now began to experience difficulties in a different quarter. When they supported Truman's firing of MacArthur and by implication the President's limited war strategy before the Congress, they attempted to do so as professional military officers. However, these issues were so interwoven with partisan politics that the Joint Chiefs of Staff became identified as administration spokesmen and exhausted their political influence. Thus, Taft insisted and Eisenhower agreed that a Republican administration must bring in a new group of chiefs.

VIETNAM

For purposes of establishing eligibility for veteran's benefits and military decorations, Vietnam officially became an American war in August 1964. However, as many studies have established, the United States was involved in Southeast Asia long before that date. For purposes of analysis, American involvement in the war in Vietnam can be broken down into three stages: gradual involvement, from 1950 to 1964; massive involvement, from 1964 to 1968; and withdrawal, from 1968 to 1973. Let us now look at the role the JCS played in each of these stages.

Gradual Involvement: 1950–1964

The United States actually became involved in Vietnam one month prior to the Korean War when Acheson decided to aid French forces in Indochina as a means of encouraging full French support for European defense. However, the first JCS position on Southeast Asia was not stated until almost two years after the outbreak of the Korean War. In a memorandum to Secretary of Defense Marshall, dated March 3, 1952, the Joint Chiefs argued that a Communist victory in Southeast Asia, or any place else in the world, directly involved a loss for the Western world.[33] However, the chiefs stopped short of recommending American military involvement in a second Asian country. It was not until the spring of 1954, one year after the Korean armistice, when the French military position in Vietnam deteriorated rapidly, that the question of intervention by American forces in that area was first broached. Along with Secretary of State Dulles, Admiral Radford, chairman of the JCS, pushed hard for direct American involvement. Radford went so far as to tell French officials that he would do his best to obtain the intervention of American carrier aircraft at Dien Bien Phu.[34]

The Eisenhower administration vacillated on the brink of intervention from April through June, when it finally became clear that the military situation had deteriorated so badly that American intervention would be useless. During the debates over intervention, one of the principal restraints on American involvement was the negative reaction of Radford's fellow chiefs, particularly Army Chief of Staff Ridgway. In May, the JCS sent a memorandum to Secretary of Defense Wilson in which they argued that, as a whole, Indochina was devoid of decisive military objectives and that the allocation of more than token American armed forces would be a serious diversion of our limited capabilities.[35] That same month, Ridgway sent a team of Army experts to Indochina to assess the situation. Their report, which Ridgway passed quickly to Eisenhower, showed that the area was particularly unsuited to our capabilities and that the cost of American intervention would be about $3.5 billion annually.[36]

However, the JCS did agree that if the decision to get involved were made, the United States should use only air and naval power from outside Indochina unless the Chinese Communists also intervened. In that eventuality, the chiefs recommended using atomic weapons against military targets in North Vietnam and China and blockading the coast of China.[37] It was clear that the JCS did not want a repeat of the Korean limited war scenario one year after we had extricated ourselves from Asia. However, this was the last time that the Joint Chiefs would serve as a brake on our involvement in Vietnam. Over the next fifteen years, the chiefs consistently advised the elected and appointed civilian officials to commit more and more resources to Southeast Asia.

After the Geneva Accords of July 1954, the United States decided to assume the burden of defending the South Vietnamese government of Ngo Dinh Diem. To accomplish this goal, the Eisenhower administration decided to send economic and military aid to Diem. The Joint Chiefs were not happy about American involvement on the side of Diem and warned that it was hopeless to expect an American military training mission to achieve success without a reasonably strong, stable civilian government in control. Moreover, the chiefs felt that the military could not do an adequate job under the 685-man limit imposed by the Geneva Accords.[38]

Despite some complaints from the military and despite the worsening situation in Vietnam, Eisenhower refused to increase the size of the military training mission beyond the limits set by the Geneva Accords. But within five months after Kennedy took over, the Joint Chiefs were pressing him for a substantial increase in the number of advisors in Vietnam.[39]

There were several interrelated reasons for the apparent turnabout of the JCS position in regard to American involvement in Vietnam in May 1961. First, this group of chiefs viewed Southeast Asia in a different context than had their predecessors. Since the mid-1950s, the struggle with Communism had shifted to wars of national liberation in the third world. If the Communists were to take power in South Vietnam, the chiefs feared that it could set a dangerous precedent and might encourage Communist insurgencies elsewhere. According to their chairman, Lyman Lemnitzer, the loss of South Vietnam would be a serious setback for the United States and would result in the "Free World's" losing Asia all the way to Singapore.[40] Second, the JCS was desirous of showing America's firmness to the Communists. The United States had looked anything but firm in the April 1961 Bay of Pigs fiasco. Third, the JCS was anxious to establish a logistic base and a legal precedent for the entry of American troops into the area before the situation in South Vietnam deteriorated too much. The chiefs did not want a repeat of the Laotian situation where the non-Communist position was so desperate and American facilities so inadequate that the JCS felt the United States could not save the non-Communists without resorting to nuclear weapons. Finally, the

Joint Chiefs felt that a deployment to Vietnam would strengthen their case for an increase in defense spending over the restrictive ceilings of the Eisenhower period. Although the chiefs were ostensibly asking the President only to increase the size of the training mission, their real interest was in getting American combat forces into Vietnam. The Joint Chiefs were willing to accept the "training mission role" only as a pretext to avoid having Diem and certain civilian officials oppose the increased troop levels.

The JCS request was ignored by the White House until late September, when President Diem, with the concurrence of Admiral Harry Felt, CINCPAC,[41] asked Washington for a bilateral treaty and an accelerated build-up. At a hastily called meeting of the National Security Council on October 11, 1961, the Joint Chiefs of Staff advised the President that 40,000 American troops would be needed to clean up the Viet Cong and an additional 128,000 would have to be sent if North Vietnam and China intervened.[42] Kennedy decided that the matter was urgent enough to send his special assistant for military affairs, Maxwell Taylor, and the then head of the State Department's planning council, Walt Rostow, to Vietnam to assess the situation.

Taylor's report, which was delivered in November, recommended a commitment of between 5,000 to 8,000 troops. General Taylor wanted most of these forces to be logistic, but admitted that some combat troops would be necessary for defense of the logistic forces. He felt that these troops could help the Diem government cope with the floods then ravaging South Vietnam and would assure the South Vietnamese president of our readiness to join him in the event that a military showdown with the Viet Cong or North Vietnamese became necessary.[43]

The JCS, along with Secretary of Defense McNamara and Deputy Secretary Gilpatric, supported Taylor's recommendations but added four admonitions. First, the United States must commit itself to the clear objective of preventing the fall of South Vietnam.

Second, the troops recommended by Taylor were only the first step and by themselves could not tip the scales decisively. Third, the struggle could be prolonged and costly and Hanoi and Peking might intervene overtly. Fourth, the commitment could involve the use of as many as six divisions or 100,000 men.[44]

On November 22, 1961, Kennedy decided to send support troops and advisors, but no combat troops. However, these non-combatant forces would number 16,000 and the Joint Chiefs were allowed to begin planning for a combat commitment. More-over, Kennedy established a major military command in Vietnam, the Military Assistance Command, Vietnam (MACV) and ap-pointed Taylor's friend, Paul Harkins, to the post. Although the Joint Chiefs approved of Kennedy's decision to increase the num-ber of Americans in Vietnam, they felt that much more needed to be done. Thus, in early January 1962, they sent a memorandum to McNamara and Kennedy outlining their feelings. The chiefs asked the civilian leaders to once again consider their recommen-dations of the previous May to deploy suitable American forces to Vietnam. The chiefs warned that a failure to do so would merely extend the date when such action must be taken and that the ulti-mate task would become proportionately more difficult.[45]

Despite the chiefs' dire predictions of impending doom, Ken-nedy's dispatch of advisors seemed, at least for 1962, to have stemmed the tide in Vietnam. In March 1962, Secretary McNa-mara, two members of the JCS, Harkins, and Frederick Nolting, our ambassador to South Vietnam, gathered in Honolulu to assess the situation, and all agreed that it looked encouraging. In Decem-ber of that year, General Earl Wheeler, the Army Chief of Staff, journeyed to Vietnam to evaluate the situation first hand. He too returned with a favorable report for his fellow chiefs. Wheeler went so far as to say that based on the progress made in 1962, it was not too optimistic to project that the insurgency could be brought under control by the end of 1965.[46] Admiral Felt at CINCPAC also predicted victory within three years. In his last state of the union message, delivered on January 14, 1963, President Kennedy proclaimed that the spearpoint of aggression had been blunted in Vietnam.

Later analysis showed that such optimism resulted from biased reporting by the Military Assistance Command in Vietnam. Taylor, who was now chairman of the JCS, had instructed Harkins to be optimistic in his reporting and the field commander had instructed his subordinates accordingly. Army Colonel John Paul Vann, who was aware that Harkins was presenting a distorted view, attempted to brief the Joint Chiefs on the true situation after his return from Vietnam, but Taylor, on the advice of Harkins, had him taken off the JCS agenda on July 8, 1963.[47]

Although South Vietnamese forces may have been making apparent statistical progress in the field, political decay was setting in rapidly in the capital. The government of Diem was becoming daily more remote, aggressive, and corrupt. The actual spark of revolt was struck in Hue on May 8, 1963, when government troops fired into a crowd of Buddhists displaying religious banners in defiance of a Diem decree. During the summer, mass demonstrations and immolations took place all over the country. The American government tried in vain to persuade Diem to meet some of the Buddhist demands. By late August, South Vietnamese army generals, who were conspiring against Diem, sought official American support.

Members of the Kennedy administration were divided over the question of cooperating in the overthrow of the South Vietnamese president. Roger Hilsman and Averell Harriman from the State Department were the prime movers of the forces opposed to Diem, while Maxwell Taylor, the chairman of the JCS, strongly objected to American approval of a coup against the Saigon leader. The debate in Washington was mirrored in Saigon, where Ambassador Lodge and General Harkins were divided over the question of the coup. During the debate in Washington, Taylor kept Harkins informed of what was happening and instructed the field commander on how to color his reports to Washington in order to buttress the case for keeping Diem.[48]

In an attempt to resolve the conflict over Diem, Kennedy dispatched McNamara and Taylor to Saigon in September 1963. Their report attempted to bridge the Harkins-Lodge gap by recommending that the United States work with but not give economic aid to Diem until he instituted certain reforms. The President decided to defer to the advice of the man on the scene and gave considerable leeway to Lodge in dealing with the plotters. The White House placed only two constraints on Lodge: he was not to become actively involved in the coup, and he was to discourage any plots which did not have a likely chance of quick success. An October coup was thwarted by Harkins' admonitions to the coup leader, but on November 1, 1963, Diem was overthrown and assassinated.

Diem's overthrow led to political chaos in Saigon and a near collapse of the military effort. While the military leaders played musical chairs in the capital, the insurgents made large gains in the field. Moreover, for a brief moment after Diem's death, officers in the field were able to report honestly about the war. The embassy in Saigon was startled by the reality of the situation and Lodge was on his way to Washington to report the gravity of the allied position when President Kennedy was assassinated.

President Johnson was thus faced with the decision of escalating the war or seeing the insurgency succeed. The Joint Chiefs recommended that the new President take a series of bold actions in Vietnam. These actions included bombing key North Vietnamese targets, sending American ground combat troops to South Vietnam, and employing United States forces as necessary in direct action against North Vietnam. Initially, Johnson was disposed toward steps that might reverse the situation but would not commit this country directly to combat. Therefore, he approved an elaborate program of covert military actions against North Vietnam, which the JCS formulated in "Operation Plan 34 A." These operations ranged from flights over North Vietnam by U-2 planes and kidnappings of North Vietnamese citizens for intelligence information, to parachuting sabotage and psychological warfare teams into the North, commando raids from the sea to blow up rail and highway bridges, and the bombardment of North Vietnamese installations by patrol boats. These destructive undertakings were begun in February 1964, and were directed by the Joint Chiefs through the office of the special assistant to the JCS for counterinsurgency and special activities. The Joint Chiefs themselves periodically evaluated the operations for McNamara. Although the chiefs were in favor of these operations, which were initially proposed by McNamara, they warned the secretary that it would be idle to conclude that they would have a decisive effect on Hanoi's will to aid the Vietcong.[49]

The "34 A" operations had little effect, and by mid-March 1964 the situation was unquestionably worse. On March 17, 1964, President Johnson directed the JCS to proceed energetically to draw up plans that would enable the United States to launch retaliatory air strikes against North Vietnam on seventy-two hours notice and full scale air raids on thirty days notice. In mid-April, the JCS approved CINCPAC's "Operation Plan 37-64," which tabulated how many planes and what bomb tonnages would be required for each phase of the air strikes. By mid-June the JCS had refined CINCPAC's plan to the point of producing a comprehensive list of ninety-four targets in North Vietnam.[50]

In June the principals once again gathered at CINCPAC headquarters in Hawaii to evaluate the situation. Although all agreed that the situation in Vietnam was growing worse, the majority were inclined against further escalation. General Taylor, speaking on behalf of the JCS, warned the conferees that there was a danger of reasoning ourselves into inaction, and that from a military point of view, the United States could now function in Southeast Asia about as well as anywhere in the world except Cuba.[51] However, on his return from Hawaii, McNamara recommended to the President that major actions could be delayed for some time yet.

In late July, at a National Security Council meeting called to discuss the progressively deteriorating situation in South Vietnam, the Joint Chiefs proposed air strikes by unmarked planes flown by non-American crews against several targets in North Vietnam, including the coastal bases for Hanoi's flotilla of torpedo boats.[52] Before any action was taken on the JCS recommendation, the controversial incidents in the Gulf of Tonkin took place. These incidents brought about a turning point in our involvement in Vietnam. No longer would American actions be on a very small scale. Within six months after the events in the Gulf, the United States would be engaged in the full-scale air campaign against North Vietnam that the JCS had long advocated.

However, no matter what steps the administration took, the chiefs would not be satisfied. They kept asking for more and more military activity, and four years later, at the time of the Tet offensive, when the United States had nearly 600,000 men in South Vietnam and had dropped more bombs on North Vietnam than this nation had dropped in all of World War II, the Joint Chiefs of Staff were still asking for increased levels of military activity.

Massive Involvement: 1964–1968

The controversial incidents in the Gulf of Tonkin took place in early August, 1964. On August 2, North Vietnamese patrol boats engaged the American destroyer *Maddox* and, on the morning of August 4, they allegedly attacked the *Maddox* and her sister ship, the *Turner Joy*. Minutes after the second incident, McNamara convened a meeting of the Pentagon to discuss the possibilities for retaliation. Secretary of State Rusk, his assistant, William Bundy, and the JCS were in attendance. All agreed to recommend reprisal air strikes to the President, and while the civilian officials were informing the President of their agreement, the JCS selected four torpedo boat bases and one air storage depot as the reprisal targets. Within six hours after the second incident, McNamara approved the reprisal order, which had been prepared by the Joint Staff.

The reprisal order was not the only directive sent to American forces that night of August 4, 1964. The Pentagon also told its forces to implement the details of OPLAN 37-64: aircraft were pre-positioned in preparation for a sustained air war against North Vietnam. The decision to begin preparation for the sustained air war was arrived at during a meeting between McNamara and the JCS on the afternoon of August 4. The secretary viewed it as a precautionary move, while the Joint Chiefs felt that it was one more step toward their ultimate goal of applying massive air power against North Vietnam.[53] Indeed, within days of the Gulf of Tonkin incidents, the JCS advised the President that an air campaign was essential to prevent a complete collapse of the American position in Southeast Asia, and the chiefs suggested the initiation of a "provocation strategy," that is, that the United States immediately undertake steps to provoke the North Vietnamese into taking actions which could then be answered by a systematic American air campaign. The Joint Chiefs felt that attempts should be made to repeat the Tonkin Gulf clashes as a pretext for escalation.[54]

The JCS position on the air war received support from several quarters. One week after the reprisal attacks, Taylor, who by now had succeeded Lodge as United States ambassador to Saigon, cabled Secretary of State Dean Rusk that the Khanh regime had only a 50-50 chance of lasting out the year and that a major objective of the mission in Saigon was to be prepared to implement contingency plans against North Vietnam by January 1, 1965. In response to Taylor's cable, William Bundy, the assistant secretary

THE OPERATIONAL ROLE   [159

of state for Far Eastern affairs, drew up a memorandum for the President which outlined a series of graduated steps toward a possible full-scale air war to begin on the date suggested by Taylor. On August 17, 1964, Admiral Sharp (CINCPAC) told the Joint Chiefs that he agreed with the idea of a full-scale air war against North Vietnam; however, Sharp urged the JCS not to lose the momentum of August 4 and recommended that the full-scale air strikes be initiated immediately. By the end of August, Assistant Secretary of Defense McNaughton had outlined several means of provocation that could culminate in a sustained air war.[55]

The President, who was in the midst of a campaign in which he had assumed the posture of a peace candidate, ordered a number of interim measures which were designed to assist the morale of the South Vietnamese and to show the Communists that we meant business, but which avoided direct large-scale American involvement. These measures were essentially a return to the clandestine measures outlined in "34 A." However, within the next few months, the Viet Cong took a series of steps that many people in Washington interpreted as provocations.

On November 1, the Viet Cong launched a devastating mortar barrage on American planes and facilities at Bienhoa. The JCS told McNamara that this attack was a deliberate act of escalation and a change of the ground rules under which the Viet Cong had operated up until then. The Joint Chiefs asserted that a prompt and strong response was clearly justified. They advocated an all-out air campaign against the North, including B-52 attacks, and the introduction of Marine and Army units into South Vietnam to provide increased security for American personnel and installations. Since November 1 was election eve, Lyndon Johnson, the peace candidate, elected to do nothing at that time. On Christmas Eve 1964, the Viet Cong planted a bomb in the American officers' quarters in Saigon. Again the JCS pressed for reprisal air strikes against the North. Despite the fact that this time the chiefs were supported vigorously in their recommendations by Taylor in Saigon and Sharp in Honolulu, the President again decided not to escalate.[56]

The JCS would not be denied thrice. When the Viet Cong attacked the U.S. military advisors' compound at Pleiku on February 6, 1965, President Johnson decided to give "an appropriate and fitting response" by launching a retaliatory strike with forty-nine Navy jets. When the guerrillas attacked an American barracks at Quinhon on February 11, the President launched the sustained air war against North Vietnam, which came to be known as "Operation Rolling Thunder."

While the Joint Chiefs had unanimously recommended an air campaign against the North, they were initially divided over the manner in which it should be conducted. John McConnell, the Air Force Chief of Staff, wanted a short and violent twenty-eight-day campaign that would begin in the southern part of North Vietnam and work its way progressively north. During these twenty-eight days, all ninety-four targets on the list drawn up by the JCS would be destroyed and all of the planes in our air arsenal, even the giant B-52s, would be employed. The other chiefs endorsed a "line of communication (LOC) cut" proposal made by Admiral Sharp. This program would have American planes first destroy all the roads and rail lines in North Vietnam to isolate her from China and force her to supply the South by sea. The United States would then bomb North Vietnam's port facilities. Eventually the chiefs envisioned bombing industries outside populated areas, and finally Hanoi and Haiphong if necessary.

However, the Joint Chiefs realized that their ability to influence the bombing campaign would be diminished if they could not agree on a common policy. Therefore, McConnell abandoned his proposal when the other chiefs incorporated some of his individual target concepts into their LOC plan.[57] In spite of the fact that the JCS thus unanimously endorsed this long-range bombing proposal, it was not accepted. In the early stages of the air war, the President retained almost complete daily control over attack concepts and target selection. Eventually the President was forced to select the targets in weekly packages and allow the on-the-scene commanders to select the precise timing of the individual attacks. Decisions on targets, type of bombs, and flight plans for the aircraft were made at the Tuesday luncheons at the White House.[58] Besides the President, Rusk, McNamara, Helms (the CIA director), and Rostow (the National Security advisor) were regular attendees. No military man was included until the summer of 1967, when Chairman Wheeler was added. Lyndon Johnson never relinquished or delegated control over the air war to anyone outside the White House. For the duration of his term, he remained the target officer. But the President eventually did approve almost all of the ninety-four targets on the JCS list, but at a pace much too slow to satisfy the Joint Chiefs.

"Rolling Thunder" operations had almost no effect on the war in the South, and a few weeks after the initiation of the bombing campaign, the military leaders began to bombard the President from all directions with requests for the introduction of large numbers of American combat troops into South Vietnam. Within ten days after the start of the sustained air war, General Westmoreland asked for two Marine battalions to guard the air base at Danang. On March 12, 1965, Harold K. Johnson, the Army Chief of Staff, after making a fact-finding trip to Vietnam, recommended the dispatch of one American division to hold coastal enclaves and defend the Central Highlands, and the creation of a four-division force of American and SEATO troops to patrol the demilitarized zone and Laotian border areas.

On March 20, the JCS, as a body, proposed sending two American divisions and one South Korean division to South Vietnam for offensive combat operations. The next week General Westmoreland submitted a request for seventeen maneuver battalions (almost two divisions) and added that more troops would be required if the bombing continued to fail to slow down infiltration.[59]

President Johnson turned down the largest of these requests. He sent only four Marine battalions for base security and increased support forces by 20,000. Johnson's decision was supported by Ambassador Taylor, who felt the South Vietnamese would resent the presence of too many foreign troops. Moreover, the ambassador did not believe that there was any military necessity for them. However, Taylor broadly interpreted the role of the Marines providing base security and allowed them to mount mobile counterinsurgency operations anywhere within fifty miles of the base, thus making them combat troops.[60]

Although the Joint Chiefs did not get their three division plan approved, they asked for and received permission from McNamara to go ahead and start planning for the introduction of three divisions and then decided to try to use the increase in support troops as a way of actually putting in more combat troops. For example, one of the "support" units which they ordered in was the 173rd Airborne Brigade, one of the Army's crack combat outfits, which Westmoreland had long coveted. When Taylor and the civilian officials in the Department of Defense became aware of the Joint Chiefs' action, the brigade was already en route to Vietnam. The ambassador protested but McNamara reluctantly approved the deployment of the brigade fifteen days after it had arrived in Vietnam.[61]

The deployment of units like the 173rd and the mobile counterinsurgency operations of the Marines committed the United States to a major combat role and established a precedent which would make it easier for the administration to approve the larger and larger requests that would soon come from Westmoreland and the JCS.

On April 20, 1965, the principals once again gathered in Honolulu to assess the situation. At the time of this meeting, there were only 40,000 American troops in Vietnam. The conferees agreed to raise the level to 82,000 and recommended seeking 7,250 additional troops from Australia and South Korea. Ten days after the conclusion of the conference, the JCS presented a detailed plan for deployment of 48,000 American and 5,250 third country forces. Before the President could respond to these requests, enemy activity had increased to such an extent that General Westmoreland felt it necessary to request a staggering total of forty-four battalions, or nearly five divisions, and a free hand to maneuver the troops.

The size of his request, which reached Washington on June 7, startled even the Joint Chiefs, who had never advocated more than three divisions or twenty-seven battalions. The chiefs even asked Sharp exactly what Westmoreland intended to do with all those troops.[62] Although they thought Westmoreland's request somewhat excessive, the Joint Chiefs did not wish to overrule the field commander. Thus, they ratified it, and, when Secretary McNamara voiced no objection, the President, in July 1965, approved the immediate dispatch of forty-four battalions, or nearly 200,000 men, to Vietnam. Moreover, the President also granted the Military Assistance Command in Vietnam freedom to maneuver the troops. Westmoreland used this permission to initiate his disastrous search-and-destroy strategy of attrition, which emphasized controlling territory rather than population. Neither McNamara nor the Joint Chiefs were overly enthusiastic about this strategy, but at that time they were unwilling to prescribe battlefield tactics from 7,000 miles away.

The United States was now committed to a major ground war and the mood in Washington was to give the field commander whatever he felt was needed. Thus, in the summer of 1965, the air war was being run from the White House and the ground war by Saigon. The Joint Chiefs were caught in between with little control over Johnson or Westmoreland but with seeming responsibility for the actions of both. This position was to prove quite disconcerting to the chiefs, and coupled with the frustrations of the political and budgetary processes, would lead them to talk of a mass resignation within two years.

President Johnson's decision to make a major commitment of American ground troops to South Vietnam was followed by a decision in Hanoi to increase the level of infiltration and led Westmoreland to ask for larger and larger numbers of American troops. His June request for forty-four battalions envisioned a total U.S. force of about 200,000 men. One month later Westmoreland asked for 275,000. By the end of 1965, the field commander has raised his estimate to 443,000, and one year after Johnson approved the forty-four battalions, Westmoreland was demanding 542,000 troops.

The JCS approved each of the Saigon commander's requests, and at each step of the escalation assured their Commander-in-Chief that South Vietnam was the linchpin of Southeast Asia.[63] However, the Joint Chiefs were bitterly disappointed that in approving Westmoreland's mammoth requests the President did not put the country on a wartime footing and call up the reserves. The thing that the chiefs feared most was a "political" war and a partial commitment. Nonetheless, rather than be overruled and provoke the President's displeasure, they went along with Johnson's strategy within the councils of government. But their true feelings were often leaked to the press or to congressional hawks. Only the brilliant negotiations of their chairman, Earl Wheeler, kept several of them from actually resigning.[64]

The Joint Chiefs did attempt to make the President aware of their perception of the realities of the situation. In June 1965, they advised the President that it would take 750,000 to 1 million men and seven or eight years to drive the Viet Cong out of South Vietnam and that a major force would have to remain there for twenty to thirty years to insure the victory. The JCS also told the Commander-in-Chief that the United States could not win in South Vietnam unless it demonstrated the will to win by appropriate strategy and tactics, by widening the air war and denying sanctuaries to the enemy.[65]

The President scoffed at the JCS figures of 1 million men and twenty to thirty years to insure a victory, but when General Wheeler asked if he had a more limited objective in mind, the President did not answer directly. Nor did he ever tell the military leaders what his objective was. McGeorge Bundy was later to lament that the administration never told the military what to do or how to do it. He stated that throughout the war there was "a premium on imprecision."[66] However, the President did allow the military to take some steps to enlarge the war. He gradually increased the number of targets in North Vietnam and allowed Westmoreland to conduct small-scale ground operations against the Communist sanctuaries in Cambodia and Laos beginning in September 1965.[67]

While Westmoreland, the Joint Chiefs of Staff, and the President were grappling over troop levels, mobilization, Communist sanctuaries, and bombing targets, the Secretary of Defense apparently was more concerned with good management than with strategy.[68] Robert McNamara spent most of 1965 carefully and personally insuring that the Department of Defense was ready to provide efficient and sufficient support to the fighting elements in Vietnam. The secretary supported the air war and the ground troop buildup because he felt that these steps would convince Hanoi of America's will and would force the Communists to negotiate. It was inconceivable to him that North Vietnam would refuse to recognize reality and continue to fight.[69]

However, by mid-1966, McNamara came to the somewhat painful conclusion that neither the bombing nor the troop buildup were improving the allied position and, beginning in late 1966, he sought to set limits to our commitment and attempted to persuade the President to seek a political settlement. The Joint Chiefs were adamant in opposing their boss and attempted to counter him by pressing Johnson to expand the war drastically. The JCS advocated bombing North Vietnam's petroleum oil and lubrication (POL) facilities, and Hanoi's locks, dams, and rail yards; urged the expansion of America's troops in South Vietnam to 700,000;

166] THE JOINT CHIEFS OF STAFF

recommended the invasion of Laos, Cambodia, and North Vietnam; and pleaded for the mobilization of the reserves. They referred to a McNamara proposal to limit the air war to south of the 20th parallel as an "aerial Dien Bien Phu"; they advised the President that if Westmoreland did not get 700,000 men, the Military Assistance Command in Vietnam would lose its momentum; and they finally threatened to resign if the President adopted McNamara's plans to reduce the level of our activity in Southeast Asia.[70]

At first President Johnson tried to steer a mid-course between the secretary and the JCS, but little by little he began to lean more and more toward the chiefs' position. "Rolling Thunder" was expanded fifty-seven times and eventually all but twelve of the targets proposed by the JCS were bombed. Troop levels in Vietnam kept expanding and General Wheeler was invited to all of the Tuesday lunches. Finally, in mid-1967, the President announced the impending dispatch of McNamara to the World Bank and commenced to look for a "real hawk" to lead the Pentagon in the war.

The Withdrawal: 1968–1973

As 1968 began, it appeared that the massive involvement had finally begun to turn the tide in South Vietnam. Reports from Westmoreland to the JCS indicated that slowly but surely real progress was being made. Then came the Tet Offensive, which began on January 31, 1968. Despite public statements to the contrary, the offensive, in which the Communists simultaneously attacked all of the major cities and towns in South Vietnam, caught the White House by surprise, and the strength, length, and intensity of the attack prolonged the shock.

The Joint Chiefs were quick to see in the offensive an opportunity to make another attempt to gain presidential acceptance of two of their most cherished objectives: an almost unlimited air campaign, and the call-up of the reserves. Thus, within four days of the initiation of the Tet attacks, the chiefs had taken two steps. First, the JCS urged the President to severely reduce the radius of the zone in which bombing was prohibited in Hanoi and Haiphong. Second, the chiefs asked Westmoreland if he needed any reinforcements and told him not to feel bound by earlier troop ceilings, because the United States was not prepared to accept defeat in Vietnam.[71]

The request to enlarge the bombing zones was turned down by the President because he felt that the larger area would include only a small number of fixed targets not previously authorized. The question of additional troops was not so easily handled. Rather, it set into motion a whole series of events that would eventually culminate in a decision to seek a negotiated settlement in Vietnam. The Joint Chiefs of Staff would play a key role during this drama. Their attempt to expand the American commitment would not only fail but also would galvanize those forces within the administration who were opposed to the war.

When Westmoreland replied that he would welcome reinforcements, the JCS recommended that no additional troops be sent to Vietnam unless the reserves were called up. Thus, when McNamara ordered 10,500 men to Vietnam on February 13, the chiefs demanded the call-up of 46,300 reservists to replace and sustain this deployment. When this request was turned down, Wheeler journeyed to Vietnam to make an on-the-scene evaluation and to consult with Westmoreland personally. His written report, which was delivered to the President on the last day of February, 1968, stated that he and Westmoreland agreed that the present troop level of 525,000 was inadequate and that 206,756 new soldiers were needed by the end of the year. In order to provide this many troops for Vietnam, Wheeler and the other chiefs urged the call-up of 280,000 reservists.[72]

The President then asked Clark Clifford, the new Secretary

of Defense and a reputed hawk, to gather a senior group of advisors to examine the domestic implications of the Wheeler-Westmoreland request, that is, how to give Westmoreland what he wanted with fairly acceptable domestic consequences. Clifford however, turned the sessions into a complete reassessment of our Vietnam policy. The reassessment turned into a three-week battle between the President's advisors over the future course of American involvement in Southeast Asia.[73] The Joint Chiefs were the principal spokesmen for stepping up that involvement drastically. They argued that not to give Westmoreland his 206,000 additional men would be tantamount to a vote of no confidence in the field commander. Moreover, the JCS urged an extension of the bombing, mining of Haiphong, and bombardment of North Vietnam with naval gunfire up to the Chinese buffer zone. However, when Clifford questioned the JCS on the effect of these additional steps, the secretary felt that the chiefs' answers were vague and unsatisfactory. They were not able to promise victory but could state only that the additional troops and actions against North Vietnam would add to the cumulative weight of our pressure on the enemy.

The JCS position did have some impact on the group. In its report, the task force recommended immediate deployment of 22,000 troops and a reserve call-up of 262,000 men. However, they reserved judgment on the remaining 185,000 men, and disagreed over the extent to which the bombing of North Vietnam should be intensified. When Clifford presented the report to the President, he dissented from its conclusions. The new secretary argued that we had accomplished our aim in South Vietnam and should begin now to disengage. Johnson was shocked by this advice from his hawkish secretary and formed a senior advisory group composed of men who had served in high government posts for the past twenty years to make an additional study. These "wise men" were briefed on the situation and, with a few exceptions, agreed that our present policy had reached an impasse, that the United States could not achieve its objectives without the application of virtually unlimited resources, and that the war was no longer being supported by a majority of the American people. They therefore recommended a significant change. General Wheeler argued that if the "wise men" had derived their views from their briefings, the briefers must have been men who did not know the true situation. Dean Acheson, one of the "wise men," responded to Wheeler's contention by telling the President that he was being led down a garden path by the JCS.

On March 31, President Johnson "promoted" Westmoreland to Army Chief of Staff, stopped the bombing north of the 20th parallel, and allowed only a token troop increase in Vietnam and a very small reserve call-up at home. Throughout the remainder of 1968, Secretary Clifford sought to effect a total bombing halt, limitations on the ground war, and a start on withdrawal of American troops. The JCS objected vehemently to each of these proposals and convinced the President that he could not de-escalate further without jeopardizing our troops. However, the JCS reluctantly agreed to a total bombing halt in October 1968, on condition that the shelling of South Vietnamese cities would cease and the de-militarized zone would not be violated.[74]

The Nixon administration came into office in January 1969 determined to extricate the United States from Vietnam, but only in such a way as not to generate an outbreak of isolationism in this country and not to undermine the credibility of American commitments in other parts of the world. Therefore, the President initiated a phased withdrawal of American troops from Vietnam while simultaneously seeking to improve the capability of the South Vietnamese to take over the actual fighting, a process known as "Vietnamization." At the same time, the Nixon administration continued the negotiations in Paris, which had begun after Johnson's actions of the previous March.

The Joint Chiefs, who were denied their wish for a wider war by the Johnson administration, were also now anxious to extri-cate their forces from this "no win" situation and apply their scarce resources elsewhere. Therefore, they agreed to publicly support the President's policy of disengagement. However, the chiefs were also concerned about the safety of U.S. troops remaining in Vietnam, and in return for their support, they asked that American planes be allowed to attack the 25,000 to 30,000 Communist personnel who preyed on U.S. troops from the sanctuaries behind the Cambodian border. The President approved their request and secret heavy bombings of Cambodia were initiated on March 18, 1969, and lasted through 1970. So secret were these raids that only the JCS, the Secretary of Defense, the President, and Henry Kissinger were aware of their existence. Neither the service secretaries nor the vice-chiefs were privy to the information because of a dual reporting system devised by the JCS. The President also allowed small units to continue operating in Cambodia and Laos, and eventually permitted a full-scale invasion of those nations, Cambodia in May, 1970, and Laos in February, 1971.[75]

From 1969 to 1972, the JCS sought to push the ground rules limiting the air war against North Vietnam to their fullest extent. According to understandings reached in Paris, air activity over North Vietnam was limited to reconnaissance flights. However, if these reconnaissance planes were fired upon, their fighter escorts were permitted to bomb the facility that was doing the firing ("protective reaction" strikes). The Joint Chiefs encouraged the on-the-scene air commanders to be more aggressive and interpret broadly their existing authority. They encouraged the commanders to double the number of fighter escorts for the reconnaissance flights and to let the escorts know that the JCS would not question aiming points. The chiefs also authorized reconnaissance flights in areas where known concentrations of North Vietnamese artillery were present and encouraged commanders to use the "protective reaction" authority to make strikes on targets other than surface-to-air missile or antiaircraft sites.[76] There is little doubt that the Nixon administration at least tacitly supported this policy, for when it came to light that General Lavelle was secretly bombing North Vietnam, in obvious defiance of the ground rules, President Nixon declined to prosecute him.[77]

At the same time that the Nixon administration was conducting its secret bombings of North Vietnam and Cambodia, General Abrams was achieving remarkable success on the ground. Although American forces were withdrawing from Vietnam, Abrams went on the offensive and made control of the population his main objective. Unlike Westmoreland, who conducted multibattalion operations over remote and sparsely inhabited pieces of real estate, Abrams broke his units down into hundreds of squads and platoons, bunched his forces around the cities, and slowly pushed out through the populated areas toward the borders. Abrams also switched his tactics from attrition of the enemy to disruption of his logistic system. He correctly perceived that the logistic system was the enemy's weakest link and emphasized a high cache count rather than a high body count. By mid-1970, Abrams had achieved near complete domination of cities and populated areas.

This domination allowed the United States to permit a Communist presence in South Vietnam in the Paris Accords, something that would have caused a government collapse in 1969. Although the Joint Chiefs applauded Abrams' success, they had very little to do with it. Just as the chiefs were not responsible for the disastrous tactics of Westmoreland, they cannot claim credit for Abrams' success.[78]

In the last months of American involvement in Vietnam, the Joint Chiefs had the satisfaction of seeing two of their most consistently advocated policies adopted. In May 1972, when North Vietnam launched a major offensive in the South, President Nixon ordered the mining of Haiphong, and in December 1972, when the North Vietnamese apparently reneged on understandings with Henry Kissinger, the President ordered massive bombings of the Hanoi area. The fact that the massive bombings apparently led to a peace accord was particularly gratifying to the Joint Chiefs. They had always maintained that the Johnson administration's gradual application of air power, which was supposed to motivate Hanoi into seeking a political solution, was counterproductive. The JCS felt that gradualism needlessly extended the scope and duration of the conflict because it granted the North Vietnamese time to shore up their air defenses, disperse their military targets, and mobilize their labor force for logistical repair and movement.[79]

Despite the fact that most of the JCS recommendations were eventually adopted, the Vietnamese War was a frustrating experience for those chiefs who tried to conduct it from Washington. Earl Wheeler, who served as chairman from 1964 to 1970 and who was often caught between his civilian authorities and his fellow chiefs, came out of it an exhausted and depleted man, his health ruined by major heart attacks. John McConnell, Harold Johnson, and David McDonald, who headed their services during the critical days of the war, are very bitter men. Although none of them has spoken out publicly, private conversations with them reveal unimaginable amounts and depths of resentment.

However, the field commanders, who publicly supported the policies made in Washington, were rewarded by promotion to the highest positions in their services. General Westmoreland, who lauded Lyndon Johnson's conduct of the war before Congress and the American people, moved from the Military Assistance Command to the Pentagon in 1968. Admiral Zumwalt, who, as commander of naval forces in Vietnam from 1968 to 1970, turned over control of naval operations in Vietnam to the South Vietnamese Navy well ahead of the administration's timetable, in July 1970 became the youngest man ever selected as Chief of Naval Operations. General Abrams, who succeeded Westmoreland as MACV and who went along with a withdrawal schedule keyed more to the 1972 elections than battlefield conditions, in 1972 became one of the oldest Army Chiefs of Staff. General George Brown, who, as commander of the 7th Air Force from 1968 to 1970, presided over many of the secret bombings of Cambodia, became the first non–Strategic Air Command oriented Air Force Chief of Staff in history when he was nominated to that position in 1973.

CONCLUSION

Before the large-scale commitment of American military forces to Korea and Vietnam, the JCS function in these situations was similar to that in the other crisis situations discussed in the first part of this chapter. The Joint Chiefs of Staff were conservative in estimating the strategic importance of both areas, very hesitant about the United States becoming involved, and in disagreement over the form of involvement. The impetus for involvement came from other agencies, and JCS endorsement of the involvement was based upon psychological rather than military grounds. Before the outbreak of war, JCS impact was minimal. However, after the introduction of American forces, leverage on the policymakers increased, and as the wars dragged on, JCS identification with the policy and the policymakers became closer and closer. In Korea the JCS supported a policy labelled as "no win" by the field commander, many congressmen, and a great part of the public. In Vietnam the JCS became advocates of a policy that continually widened the scope of the war and raised the stakes in a desperate attempt to achieve some form of victory, a policy that increasingly disenchanted larger and larger segments of the American public. During the Korean War the President fired the recalcitrant field commander and relied more and more on the JCS. During Vietnam the President fired the Secretary of Defense "when he became soft" and began to depend more heavily on the chiefs.

How are we to evaluate the part played by the Joint Chiefs of Staff in Korea and Vietnam? The performance of the Joint Chiefs can be judged by their contribution to maintaining the civil-military balance and by the responsibility which they bear for the decisions which were made. The civil-military balance during wartime may be paraphrased thusly: "If war is too important to be left to the generals, it is also too complex to leave them out of it." In Korea and Vietnam, the war was not left to the chiefs, nor were they left out. With some minor exceptions, the Joint Chiefs were not responsible for upsetting the civil-military balance in either of these conflicts. However, their relationship with civilian leaders and other military men was quite different in each war.

In Korea the JCS was a part of every major decision from the first involvement to the dismissal of MacArthur and the move toward seeking a negotiated settlement short of total victory. The Joint Chiefs and their civilian counterparts had a harmonious relationship. In their memoirs both the President and the Secretary of State have nothing but high praise for the conduct of the JCS during the Korean War. The JCS and the administration had excellent rapport because their views on the war were basically the same. Bradley's statement that Korea was "the wrong war, at the wrong time, in the wrong place, and with the wrong enemy" could have been made by any member of Truman's national security bureaucracy. More important, the JCS supported the administration position for purely military reasons. Unfortunately for the chiefs, many people were not able to separate military and partisan political considerations.

The threat to the civil-military balance in Korea came from the field commander, General MacArthur. Initially the JCS contributed to the imbalance by refusing to exercise authority over the general. However, the chiefs made up for their initial reluctance to confront MacArthur when they supported Truman's dismissal of the Far East commander. In many ways, their performance during the period immediately preceding and following Truman's decision to relieve MacArthur was their "finest hour." Given the almost fanatical support that the general had in Congress, the media, and the public, a refusal by the chiefs to defend the firing of MacArthur would have made Truman's decision more difficult, if not impossible. By their actions, the Joint Chiefs prevented a constitutional crisis and solidified the American tradition of civilian control over the military.

The Pentagon Papers make clear that JCS advice was solicited and given throughout the American involvement in Southeast Asia. The multi-volume study is replete with memoranda from the JCS on every aspect of the conflict. The chiefs did not experience difficulty with the field commander in Vietnam as they had in Korea. Westmoreland's battlefield tactics may have been questionable, but his support for administration objectives and JCS directives was never doubted. Abrams, too, was a loyal supporter of policy made in Washington. In fact, both Westmoreland and Abrams defended the administration's policies in public forums. The former even addressed a joint session of the Congress in 1967 in order to solicit support for the Johnson administration's conduct of the war.

The JCS did become involved in sometimes fierce bureaucratic struggles with certain members of the Kennedy and Johnson administrations. Throughout the war, the Joint Chiefs always wanted to expand the war more rapidly and make it more extensive than did most of their civilian counterparts. The bureaucratic infighting that resulted from this difference of opinion did lead to actions by both sides that could have upset the civil-military balance. However, subsequent reactions always restored it. Initially no member of the JCS was invited to the Tuesday lunches where bombing policy was established. As a result of negative reaction in Congress and in the press, this situation was rectified in August 1967, when Wheeler was invited and was institutionalized in the Nixon administration when the chairman was made a member of the Washington Special Action Group (WASAG). Secretary of Defense McNamara often failed to solicit JCS advice on his "dovish" proposals. However, the JCS "got the President's attention" by threatening to resign if these proposals were accepted, and Mc-Namara was forced out. But McNamara's successor, Clifford, was just as dovish and convinced the President that the United States should withdraw.

In looking at the second criteria, bearing responsibility for decisions, it must be noted that although the ultimate responsibility for wartime decisions lies with the President, much of what he does in wartime comes as a result of pressure from his military leaders. Only if he ignores or overrules their advice can the military avoid taking some of the responsibility. Such was not the case in either Korea or Vietnam. The discussions in this chapter have demonstrated that the Joint Chiefs cannot claim the role of scapegoats; they cannot claim they were singled out unjustly for the failures of our policy in both conflicts.

The JCS recommended and supported the withdrawal from Korea that precipitated the Communist attack. The chiefs urged the President to allow MacArthur to cross the 38th parallel and then refused to curb the provocative tactics of the field commander, which ultimately led to the massive Chinese intervention and near annihilation of American forces. Beginning in 1961, the JCS, accepting the ill-conceived domino theory, urged the commitment of large numbers of American ground troops into Vietnam. Throughout the early period of the Johnson administration, the Joint Chiefs importuned the chief executive to bomb North Vietnam and recommended a strategy of provocation. Once troops had been committed and the bombing begun, the JCS urged the introduction of more and more troops and heavier bombing, despite evidence that both were counterproductive.

Responsibility is a two-edged sword. The Joint Chiefs can also claim credit for some of the successes of both wars. The decision of the Truman administration to seek a negotiated settlement in Korea rather than attempting to win a military victory over the Chinese was aided and abetted by the support of the JCS. Likewise, the actions that apparently convinced the North Vietnamese to accept a negotiated settlement—the mining of Haiphong in May 1972 and the massive bombing of Hanoi in December 1972—were originally conceived by the JCS.

JCS failures and successes came close to balancing each other in Korea, but not in Vietnam. Their support of the decision to limit the war to Korea and to relieve MacArthur balanced the mistakes of the untimely withdrawal and the ill-conceived advance toward the Chinese frontier. However, the military actions which apparently convinced Hanoi to allow us to extricate ourselves from Vietnam with some semblance of dignity could never make up for the disastrous military policy which this nation followed from 1961 through 1968 and for which the JCS must share the responsibility.

In retrospect, it would have been better for the JCS, the military, and the nation if the Joint Chiefs had refused to support Johnson's war policies and resigned en masse to show their displeasure. Wheeler's negotiations, which prevented the chiefs' resignations and secured their tacit support for the President's policies, may have had some beneficial short-term effects and may have preserved the chiefs' ability to influence Johnson on future occasions. However, in the long run, the chiefs' conduct caused a great deal of harm.

If the Joint Chiefs had resigned en masse in the summer of 1965 when Lyndon Johnson decided to Americanize the Vietnam War with draftees, a national debate over Vietnam would have ensued. No member of the JCS had ever resigned, and a group resignation undoubtedly would have led both hawks and doves to question the wisdom of our Vietnamese policies. As it was, the nation slipped almost imperceptibly into a war that resulted in almost a half million casualties and over fifty thousand deaths. Although a resignation or a refusal to endorse the official policy may not have changed the course of the war, such actions may have had other beneficial aspects. For example, they may have prevented the military leaders from becoming a part of such unsavory by-products of the war as provocation strategies, protective reaction strikes, secret bombings, dual reporting systems, and misleading the public and Congress. These are activities unbefitting a group of men whose ideal is "duty, honor, and country."

While it is true that the JCS must accept responsibility for their advice and actions, one cannot place the entire blame for the Vietnamese debacle on the Joint Chiefs. Their policy assumptions and conduct were not markedly different from many of the civilian policymakers. Almost to a man, the elected politicians and career bureaucrats assumed either that Vietnam was vital to American national security or that this nation could not stand for the loss of another country to Communism.[80] Moreover, none of the civilians who opposed the war resigned because of it. Undersecretary of State George Ball remained in the administration to preserve his influence to restrain the hawks. Vice-President Humphrey became a team player after his opposition to the Americanization of the war resulted in his exclusion from the policy-making process. McGeorge Bundy, the assistant for national security affairs, Robert McNamara, and many of their subordinates became *post facto* doves after Johnson's policies proved ineffective, but they were initially loyal supporters of American intervention. Some of these men paid a heavy price for their support of the administration's policies. For one man, Hubert Humphrey, the price was the Presidency in 1968. Likewise, the Joint Chiefs of Staff and the military suffered a great deal over Vietnam. In the early 1960s, the JCS urged intervention by our armed forces in Vietnam to save that nation from Communism, but by the late 1960s they advocated withdrawal to save the armed forces, which were racked by drugs, dissension, corruption, war crimes, and racism. The question that must be faced now is whether the Joint Chiefs of Staff are capable of providing the leadership needed to restore the military to its proper place.

CHAPTER FIVE

★

Conclusion

At various times during their first twenty-five years, the Joint Chiefs of Staff have been accused, sometimes simultaneously, of dominating American foreign policy on the one hand and of being weak, divided, and never consulted on the other. As the preceeding analysis has indicated, these types of allegations are absurd. However, such charges continue to be hurled at the JCS,[1] primarily because many of the critics do not understand the origins, prerogatives, purpose, and limitations of this uniquely American structure.

The JCS evolved accidentally in the early stages of World War II. The success of the allied war machine obscured the weaknesses of the Joint Chiefs and created false expectations for their future performance. Contrary to the intentions of some of its framers, the National Security Act and its amendments did not create a unified military establishment, and the JCS is not the cause but the reflection of that diversity. The Joint Chiefs are often not unified on important issues, because they represent constituencies with divergent viewpoints. The chiefs do not have any men and material at their disposal. By themselves, they cannot even move a ship. They cannot be blamed for the battlefield disasters of MacArthur or Westmoreland. Nor can they take credit for the successful tactics of Ridgway and Abrams. The Joint Chiefs are

179

advisors and have as much power and influence as the political leaders wish to give them. If American foreign policy has been too militaristic, or if this nation has spent inordinate amounts on defense, responsibility must lie ultimately with the elected officials, who themselves are aggressively inclined or who have been too willing to follow military advice.

The Joint Chiefs of Staff often use political strategy and pressure in pursuing their goals, but so do the other actors in the bureaucratic process. If on occasion elected officials choose to ignore the chiefs or do not consult with them, this does not mean the structure is weak. Rather, it is often the case that political leaders are uncomfortable with military officials whom they did not personally select. Finally, it is true that the chiefs have shown themselves to be poor planners. However, can one expect more from men whose previous careers have been in the operational realm and to whom no one has ever given very definitive guidance?

Given the constraints placed upon them by their position in the Department of Defense and the American political system, the Joint Chiefs have performed reasonably well. Although their response to the environment generally lags for a time, they usually have been flexible enough to make the necessary adjustments before it becomes too late. As we have seen in the preceding pages, the chiefs eventually adapted to the false economies of Louis Johnson, the madness of MacArthur, the strategic absurdities of the Eisenhower administration, the management innovations and high-handedness of McNamara, and the excessive secrecy of the Nixon administration. However, there are two areas of continuing weakness.

First, the Joint Chiefs have consistently allowed themselves to be intimidated by political leaders into supporting policies to which they were or should have been opposed. At one time or another, the chiefs publicly supported Truman's very low defense budgets, Eisenhower's "New Look," McNamara's methods, Lyndon Johnson's war policies, and Nixon's secret bombings. By legitimizing these somewhat controversial policies, the military leaders clearly did a disservice to their country and their profession.

Second, for the most part, the Joint Chiefs have not shown themselves to be innovators in the policy process, even in military areas. The chiefs have generally been reactors rather than initiators. Containment, massive retaliation, Vietnamization, and détente originated in other parts of the bureaucracy. Even when a situation cries out for change, the JCS remains addicted to the status quo. Although Truman and Eisenhower made it clear that their ceilings would not be bridged, the JCS persisted in trying to get more money and essentially removed themselves from the budget process. As the war in Vietnam dragged on and on, the only prescription that the JCS could offer was more of the same. As Lyndon Johnson remarked, "Bomb, bomb, bomb, that's all you know."[2]

What of the second twenty-five years for America's military leaders? If anything, the tasks of the Joint Chiefs of Staff will be more difficult. Unlike the days immediately following World War II, when military leaders had a great deal of prestige, the post-Vietnam chiefs find themselves virtually unknown to the public. The commander of the allied forces in Europe and the first post-World War II Chief of Staff could easily be elected President, but the commander of allied forces in Vietnam and first post-Vietnam Army Chief of Staff could not even win a gubernatorial primary in South Carolina against an orthodontist.

Today's chiefs face an unfavorable and sometimes hostile environment. In real terms, defense spending has declined by over 30 percent since fiscal year 1968. Yet public opinion polls show that two thirds of the American people favor a further reduction in defense spending. Responding to this public mood, Congress annually slashes billions from Department of Defense requests and makes changes in nearly every single line item in the military budget. Between fiscal year 1969 and fiscal year 1975, the legislature slashed $22.1 billion, or 5 percent, from the military budget. In the preceding decade Congress reduced defense authority by only $1.8 billion, or 1.3 percent. Even the traditional stalwarts on the Hill, such as Senators McClellan and Stennis, have turned against the present levels of defense spending, and the new, more liberal 94th Congress is certain to be even more desirous of reducing the highly visible and controllable defense budget.[3]

The draft has been allowed to expire, and the high cost of volunteers has forced total manpower down to 2.1 million, its lowest level since the days of the near total demobilization immediately following World War II. In fiscal year 1975, $48 billion, or 55 percent, of the defense budget will be absorbed by personnel costs, and the average cost per person will be $13,500. Table 12 contains a breakdown of Defense Department costs from 1961 to 1975, which vividly demonstrates the rising costs of

TABLE 12

Outlays for the Department of Defense
by Category, 1961–1981
(in billions of dollars)

Category	1961	1964	1968	1971	1973	1975	Change	1981*
Basic Pay	7.1	8.5	12.8	16.2	17.6	19.0	11.9	21.6
Allowances	4.2	5.0	7.5	7.0	6.3	7.5	3.3	8.5
Retired	.8	1.2	2.1	3.4	4.4	6.1	5.3	7.1
Civil Service	6.4	7.3	10.3	12.2	13.0	14.9	8.5	16.8
Total Pay	18.5	22.0	32.7	38.7	41.2	47.5	29.0	54.0
Percentage	(41)	(43)	(42)	(51)	(56)	(55)	(14)	(57)
Operating	5.5	6.2	12.3	11.2	10.7	11.6	6.1	12.3
Percentage	(12)	(12)	(16)	(14)	(14)	(14)	(2)	(14)
Investment	20.6	22.6	33.1	25.7	22.9	26.7	6.1	27.8
Percentage	(46)	(45)	(42)	(35)	(30)	(31)	(−15)	(29)
Total	44.6	50.8	78.0	75.5	76.5	85.8	44.2	94.1

* In FY 1975 dollars.

manpower and the shifting priorities in defense spending. Between 1961 and 1975, Department of Defense outlays have risen by $41.2 billion in current dollars. Seventy percent of this increase has been accounted for by rising personnel costs. Investment and operating expenditures have risen by only 15 percent each over this fifteen-year period.

In spite of the high costs of personnel, the quality of the volunteer force is suspect. Drug and discipline problems abound, particularly among Army troops in Europe. In May 1974, James Cowan, the assistant secretary of defense for health and environment, admitted that drug use among troops in Europe is a "relatively serious" problem,[4] and in late 1974, the Army's European commander was forced to court-martial seven soldiers and one officer for refusing to get haircuts. Even the Marines have seething drug and racial problems at Camp Lejune and in Okinawa.[5] Recruitment problems will continue to be difficult in the future as 60 percent of this nation's young people want nothing to do with the military[6] and the number of draft-eligible men is beginning to decline.

The Defense Department's financial problems are further exacerbated by the deferred costs of the military retirement system and of inflation. The costs of the nonfunded military retirement system have risen by 300 percent since fiscal year 1968 and will necessitate outlays of over $6 billion in 1975. Since fiscal year 1964, retirement costs have gone up more than either operating or investment expenditures, and by the end of the decade retirement will cost nearly $15 billion. Inflation, coupled with technological advances and some shoddy management practices, has made most weapon systems so expensive that the services can afford to buy less and less hardware. As indicated in table 13, the cost of the twenty ongoing major procurement programs has risen by $30 billion over the past five years, almost faster than the rate at which Congress can appropriate money for these programs. Presently the cost of the manned bomber is approaching $80 million,

TABLE 13

Major Procurement Programs
(Millions of Dollars)*

Program	Total Cost	Number of Units	Unit Cost	Authorized Through FY75	Remainder	Original Estimate	Percent Increase	Completion Date
Minuteman III	6,961	550	13	5,769	1,192	4,674	49	1979
Trident (submarine)	15,446	10	1,544	3,033	12,413	12,431	24	1984
B-1 (bomber)	18,633	244	76	2,027	16,606	11,218	66	1983
AWACS (aircraft)	2,655	34	78	1,046	1,609	2,661	—**	1980
SAM-D (missile)	6,389	N/A	N/A	853	5,536	5,240	13	1990
F-14 (aircraft)	6,307	334	19	4,843	1,464	6,166	2**	1977
F-15 (aircraft)	10,941	749	15	4,135	6,806	7,355	49	1981
S-3A (aircraft)	3,289	187	18	2,675	614	2,891	14	1977
P-3C (aircraft)	2,724	220	12	1,840	884	1,294	111	1979
F-16 (aircraft)	4,300	650	7	113	4,187	3,000	43	1985
UTTAS (helicopter)	3,402	1,117	3	240	3,162	2,307	48	1986
AAH (helicopter)	2,518	481	5	130	2,388	1,800	40	1984
SSN 688 (submarine)	7,863	36	218	4,691	3,172	5,747	37	1979
MK 48 (torpedo)	1,557	2,000	1	1,072	485	1,753	—**	1979
DD 963 (destroyer)	3,599	30	120	2,778	821	2,581	39	1978
PF (patrol boat)	5,274	50	105	411	4,863	3,244	62	1984

TABLE 13 (*continued*)

Program	Total Cost	Number of Units	Unit Cost	Authorized Through FY75	Remainder	Original Estimate	Percent Increase	Completion Date
DLGN 38 (cruiser)	1,592	5	318	1,135	457	820	94	1979
XM-1 (tank)	4,275	3,312	1	101	4,174	3,005	42	1989
A-10 (aircraft)	2,733	743	4	370	2,363	2,489	10	1980
PHM (hydrofoil)	1,108	30	37	157	951	726	53	1982
Total	111,566			37,419	74,147	81,402	38	

* Assumes 11 percent inflation in fiscal year '75, 8 percent in '76, decreasing to 4.3 percent in fiscal year '80, and 3.7 percent thereafter.

** Program cost increases were held down by decreasing the number of units; for example, the number of F-14's has been cut in half.

Source: Selected Acquisition Report Program Acquisition Cost Summary June 30, 1974, Office of the Assistant Secretary of Defense (Comptroller)

a fighter plane $20 million, a destroyer $125 million, and a tank
$1 million. When these factors are coupled with the shift in de-
fense priorities outlined in table 12, the result is that the military
inventory is at historic lows; for example, for the first time since
the 1930s, the number of ships in the Navy has dropped below 500.

In addition to the difficulties in the external environment, over
which the Joint Chiefs have little control, the military leaders have
compounded the problem by some of their own activities. The
JCS developed a dual reporting system to mask the 170,000
American bombing sorties over Cambodia from the Congress and
the public. The JCS liaison officer at the White House, Rear Admiral Robert O. Welander, has been labeled by the Senate Armed
Services Committee as a cognizant participant in and given the major
responsibility for the rifling of burn bags at the National Security
Council and the pilfering of papers from Henry Kissinger's brief-
case in order to get information to the JCS.[7] Finally, the chairman
of the JCS recently made an irresponsible remark about the extent
of Jewish influence in this country. In responding to a question
at a Duke University Law School forum on October 10, 1974,
General Brown stated that the Jews have too much influence in
the Congress and control this country's banks and newspapers.
Because Brown's remarks displayed such an appalling ignorance
of the true situation, many people wondered about the intellectual
level of the chiefs, especially since Brown is reputed to be the most
intellectually competent member of the JCS.

The outlook for the future is not completely bleak. As they
begin their second twenty-five years, the Joint Chiefs do so with a
complete new cast, which is possibly the most well-rounded group
of men ever to sit on the JCS. Not since Eisenhower brought in a
whole new set of chiefs in the summer of 1953 has there been so
great a turnover on the JCS and such a complete break with the
past. Between July and September of 1974, Presidents Nixon and
Ford were able to make four new appointments to this body. The
vacancies occurred because of the simultaneous expiration of the

terms of Admirals Moorer and Zumwalt and the untimely death of General Abrams.

The chairman of the JCS is 56-year-old former Air Force Chief of Staff General George Brown. He is the first Air Force officer to hold the post since General Twining retired in 1959. Brown was the personal choice of Secretary of Defense Schlesinger. The secretary selected Brown because his extensive experience in the joint arena and his broadly diversified Air Force career made him uniquely qualified for the top position. Moreover, the general's outlook closely parallels that of Schlesinger. Both Brown and Schlesinger are analytical conservatives who believe in the global military mission of the United States but who are not inclined to overstate the Soviet military threat or understate American military capabilities. For example, even though the Soviet Union has undertaken a vast expansion of its intercontinental ballistic missile program, both Brown and Schlesinger remain confident that the Russians cannot demolish the Air Force's deterrent force of land-based Minutemen intercontinental missiles.

Brown's choice for his successor as Air Force Chief of Staff is 53-year-old General David Jones. Like Brown, Jones has had a broadly diversified Air Force career. A native of South Dakota and a former aviation cadet, Jones has served with training, rescue, and refueling squadrons and has commanded units of the Strategic Air Command and the Tactical Air Command. He has spent time in the Pentagon, in Europe and Asia, and has attended the National War College. Jones was an aide to Curtis Lemay at the Strategic Air Command and was Brown's deputy in Vietnam. He did not see action in World War II, but he flew twenty-nine bombing missions over North Korea and spent six months in Vietnam with the 7th Air Force. At the time of his appointment to chief, Jones was the commander of American Air Forces in Europe. He was selected by Brown because of his broad Air Force background.

The Chief of Naval Operations is 52-year-old Admiral James

Holloway III. The son of Admiral James Holloway, Jr., and an Annapolis classmate of Admiral Zumwalt, Holloway is one of the most well-rounded individuals to rise to the Navy's top spot. He was commissioned as a surface officer and saw destroyer duty in the Atlantic and Pacific theatres during World War II. After the war, Holloway entered flight training, flew fighter planes in Korea, and commanded an attack squadron in the Lebanon landings and the Quemoy-Matsu crisis. During the academic year 1961–62 he attended the National War College. In 1965 he was selected for the nuclear reactor program and spent a year studying nuclear engineering under the Navy's most distinguished submariner, Admiral Hyman Rickover. Holloway's commands have included a seaplane tender, the nuclear-powered aircraft carrier *Enterprise,* Carrier Division 6, and the entire 7th Fleet. In addition, he served as deputy commander of the Atlantic Fleet, as director of the Strike Warfare Division in the Office of the Chief of Naval Operations, and as vice-CNO and spent two tours in Vietnam. Holloway was a compromise choice for CNO. Admiral Zumwalt's personal choice to continue his revolution was 50-year-old fellow surface officer Admiral Worth Bagley. Secretary of the Navy John Warner, who was alarmed at the 80 percent turnover rate in admirals and the chaos which occurred during Zumwalt's four-year term, preferred a more traditional officer, such as 55-year-old Admiral Isaac Kidd. The CNO and the secretary agreed on Holloway, who does not support change for the sake of change, nor tradition solely for tradition's sake, and who aims to slow the Navy's rate of change, to study the new initiatives, and to work toward incorporating the successful ones more into day-to-day Navy life.[8] His fellow officers refer to him as an "enlightened traditionalist," a label which Holloway solidified by naming Admiral Bagley as his first deputy.

The present Army Chief of Staff is 58-year-old General Frederick Weyand, Abrams' alter ego in Vietnam and the Pentagon. The second Army chief in the postwar period not to have graduated from West Point, Weyand studied criminology at the University of California and graduated with an ROTC commission in 1939. Called to active duty in World War II, he served in intelligence assignments in Washington and in the China-India-Burma theater. After the war, Weyand switched to the regular Army and changed to the infantry. He was a battalion commander in Korea and headed a division and field force in Vietnam. Between the Asian wars, Weyand attended both the Armed Forces Staff College and the National War College and served as a military assistant to Secretaries of the Army Robert Stevens and Wilbur Brucker. He also spent three years with the Army in Europe, headed the Army's Legislative Liaison Office for two years, and served as an advisor to the American delegation to the Paris Peace Talks with the North Vietnamese for one year. In 1970, Abrams selected Weyand to be his deputy at the Military Assistance Command in Vietnam, and when Abrams moved up to be Chief of Staff, Weyand became the allied commander in Vietnam. After the American withdrawal from Vietnam in early 1973, Weyand spent six months as head of the United States Army in the Pacific, and, in August 1973, Abrams chose him to be his deputy in the Pentagon. Secretary of Defense Schlesinger chose Weyand to succeed Abrams because of Weyand's close association with Abrams, his similarity in views, and his broad-based background.

If any group of military officers can provide the leadership necessary for the military to adjust to post-Vietnam realities, this particular group of men or men of their caliber should be able to do so. All of the chiefs have broad backgrounds in their own services. None of these four men is identified with only one branch of a particular service. These chiefs represent the diverse sources of commissioned officers. Brown comes from West Point, Holloway from Annapolis, Weyand from ROTC, and Jones from Officers Candidate School. All of the members of the JCS attended the Joint Service National War College and all have held command at the three levels of command. None of the present chiefs is identified with a particular theater, and all of these men have served and commanded in both Europe and Asia. Finally, all of these men have had extensive prior exposure to the Washington scene.

In addition to a well-prepared group of Joint Chiefs, there are other hopeful signs. A survey conducted by the Institute for Social Research at the University of Michigan in the fall of 1973 found that among the general population the United States military is now the most admired of American institutions.[9] The new strategic arms agreement concluded by President Ford and Chairman Brezhnev in the fall of 1974 may relieve some of the upward pressure on the defense budget. The deteriorating economic situation has facilitated the recruitment and retention of volunteers for the armed forces. Military pay is now comparable to that in the private sector, and the Department of Defense should not be faced with any further massive catch-up pay raises. Finally, improvements in the Reserves should enable the weekend warriors to assume some of the burdens of defense and deterrence at a far lower cost.[10]

No one can accurately predict the nature of the international environment over the next decade or quarter of a century. Nor can one foretell the part that the JCS will play in structuring the American response. The only thing that is certain is that there will be a Joint Chiefs of Staff, composed of service chiefs and a chairman. Doubtless there will be many studies and proposals to modify and perhaps eliminate the Joint Chiefs, but if past history is any indicator, all of those proposals will have very little if any impact on this unique structure.

Appendix

INTERVIEWEES

George Anderson, Admiral USN, CNO. Interviewed September 5, 1968.

Art Barber, Deputy Assistant Secretary of Defense. Interviewed February 2, 1968.

Arleigh Burke, Admiral USN, CNO. Interviewed September 6, 1968.

George Decker, General USA, Chief of Staff. Interviewed September 4, 1968.

John McConnell, General USAF, Chief of Staff. Interviewed June 17, 1971.

David McDonald, Admiral USN, CNO. Interviewed August 27, 1968.

Wilfred McNeil, Comptroller DOD. Interviewed December 13, 1968.

Robert Moot, Comptroller DOD. Interviewed December 8, 1972.

G. Warren Nutter, Assistant Secretary of Defense. Interviewed April 18, 1973.

Arthur Radford, Admiral USN, Chairman JCS. Interviewed September 4, 1968.

Robert Sikes, Chairman of the House Subcommittee on Military Construction. Interviewed August 14, 1968.

Carl Spaatz, General USAF, Chief of Staff. Interviewed September 5, 1968.

Maxwell Taylor, General USA, Chairman JCS, Chief of Staff, Military Assistant to the President. Interviewed September 4, 1968.

Earl Wheeler, General USA, Chairman JCS, Chief of Staff. Interviewed October 8, 1971.

Notes

PREFACE

1. For contrasting views of the JCS see Maxwell Taylor, *The Uncertain Trumpet* (New York: Harper, 1959), p. 80, and Stuart Loory, *Defeated* (New York: Random House, 1973), p. 95

2. The most recent panel to criticize the JCS was President Nixon's Blue Ribbon Defense Panel. Wilfred J. McNeil, the only man on the panel with previous experience in the Department of Defense, dissented from the panel's criticisms of the JCS. For the complete report see *Report to the President and the Secretary of Defense on the Department of Defense,* July 1, 1970.

3. For example: Samuel Huntington, *The Soldier and the State* (Cambridge: Harvard University Press, 1959); Paul Hammond, *Organizing for Defense* (Princeton: Princeton University Press, 1961); Morris Janowitz, *The Professional Soldier* (Glencoe: The Free Press, 1960).

4. For example: William Kaufmann, *The McNamara Strategy* (New York: Harper, 1964) and John Ries, *The Management of Defense* (Baltimore: The Johns Hopkins Press, 1965).

5. For example: Ward Just, *Military Men* (New York: Knopf, 1970); Adam Yarmolinsky, *The Military Establishment* (New York: Harper, 1971); James Donovan, *Militarism USA* (New York: Scribner, 1970); and Stuart Loory, *Defeated.*

6. For example: Donald Bletz, *The Role of the Military Professional in U.S. Foreign Policy* (New York: Praeger, 1972) and Haynes Johnson and George Wilson, *Army in Anguish* (New York: Pocket Books, 1972).

CHAPTER ONE: AN OVERVIEW

1. House Committee on Appropriations, *Hearings on the Fiscal Year 1957 Defense Budget,* Volume I, p. 547.

2. Eugene Zuckert, "The Service Secretary: Has He A Useful Role?" *Foreign Affairs,* April 1966, p. 470.

3. Zuckert, "The Service Secretary," p. 471.

4. Paul Schratz, "The McNamara Revolution," *The American Secretaries of the Navy,* Naval Institute (forthcoming).

5. Connally served as Secretary of the Navy for less than eleven months and Stahr as Secretary of the Army for seventeen months.

6. Four chiefs (Vandenberg, Burke, McConnell, and Wheeler) have had their terms extended; three (Denfeld, Anderson, and Lemay) were let go before completion of a normal tour. The only presidential appointee to have difficulty with the Senate was General Creighton Abrams. His appointment was delayed for three months while the Senate investigated his involvement in the Lavelle Affair (see chapter four for a complete discussion of the incident).

7. U.S., Statutes at Large, LXI, 253, Sec. 211; LXI, 875, Sec. 211; LXIII, 203, Sec. 1; and LXIII, 579.

8. "JCS: Organization and Functions," *Commanders Digest,* June 14, 1973, p. 4.

9. Dwight Eisenhower, *Waging Peace* (Garden City: Doubleday, 1965), p. 356.

10. Admiral John McCain, CINCPAC, from 1968 to 1972 was senior to Admiral Zumwalt, the CNO.

11. Testimony of General Wheeler to Senate Armed Services Committee on July 30, 1971. The *New York Times,* July 31, 1973, pp. 1 and 4.

12. See chapter four for a discussion of this incident.

13. Despite the familiarity with JCS procedures that one would apparently acquire in this position, only one director, Earl Wheeler, has moved up to the JCS.

14. Two operations deputies, Harold Johnson and Thomas White, have moved up to the JCS.

15. For a complete account of JCS activities in World War II, see William Leahy, *I Was There* (New York: McGraw Hill, 1950). Admiral Leahy was the wartime chairman.

16. Leahy, *I Was There,* p. 150.

17. Paul Hammond, *Organizing for Defense* (Princeton University Press, 1961), pp. 166–170.

18. In his last report to Congress, Laird complained about service parochialism and spoke about the need for a new order of service partnership. *Annual Defense Department Report FY 1973,* February

17, 1972, pp. 17–18. Forrestal's remarks are contained in *Report of the Secretary 1948.*

19. *Report to the President and the Secretary of Defense on the Department of Defense,* July 1, 1970, and *Report of the Commission on the Organization of the Executive Branch of Government,* 1949.

20. Paul Hammond, "Supercarriers and B-36 Bombers," in *American Civil-Military Decisions* (Tuscaloosa: University of Alabama Press, 1963).

21. See chapter four for a discussion of this incident.

22. Interview.

23. Interview.

24. Curtis Lemay, *Mission with Lemay* (Garden City: Doubleday, 1965), and Maxwell Taylor, *The Uncertain Trumpet* (New York: Harper, 1960) are excellent sources of the internal procedures of the JCS.

25. Interview.

26. "JCS: Organization and Functions," *Commanders Digest,* June 14, 1973, p. 2.

27. Deputy Chief of Staff for Plans.

28. Named after the color and texture of the reports prepared at various stages of the process.

29. See chapter three for a discussion of this phenomenon.

30. David Halberstam, *The Best and the Brightest* (New York: Random House, 1972), p. 564.

CHAPTER TWO· THE MEN

1. Data on members of the JCS were obtained from their official biographies, which were supplied by their respective information offices, from *Current Biography, Who's Who in America,* and from interviews.

2. Morris Janowitz, *The Professional Soldier* (Glencoe: The Free Press, 1960), p. 89.

3. For example, see Robert Heinl, "Schlesinger Angers Services: Takes Control of Promotions," *Armed Forces Journal,* October 1974, p. 23.

4. Quoted in Trudi Mc C. Osborne, "Peter Dawkins, All-American Military Man," *Washington Post/Potomac,* December 8, 1974, p. 34.

5. There are two levels of postgraduate training available to military officers: staff college and war college. Each of the services has

its own schools and there are joint colleges under the supervision of the JCS. The Army and the JCS separate their colleges physically while the Navy and Air Force have both staff and warfare colleges in the same location. The Army has its Command and General Staff College in Fort Leavenworth, Kansas, and its War College in Carlisle, Pennsylvania. The Navy has both courses at its War College in Newport, Rhode Island, and the Air Force has both courses at the Air University in Montgomery, Alabama. The "joint" Armed Forces Staff College is located in Norfolk, Virginia, and the National War College is in Washington, D.C.

6. This school is no longer in existence. It has been replaced by the Industrial College of the Armed Forces, which trains officers in resource management.

7. Each of the services admits small numbers of officers from the other services to their own colleges.

8. For example, the new Trident submarine program will cost $15 billion.

9. Dwight Eisenhower, *Waging Peace* (Garden City: Doubleday, 1965), p. 356.

10. Zumwalt had great difficulty in getting members of the naval hierarchy to support his reforms fully. The race riots aboard Navy ships were one result of this lack of enthusiasm for Zumwalt's changes.

11. Anderson was appointed as ambassador to Portugal when he was relieved as CNO.

12. Anderson was selected for rear admiral while serving as a special assistant to the chairman of the JCS.

13. A Senate Armed Services Committee report on the incident subsequently placed the major responsibility for the surreptitious activity on Rear Admiral Robert O. Welander, the head of the JCS liaison office in the White House. The committee found that Admiral Moorer did nothing improper in connection with the entire episode. *New York Times,* December 22, 1974, p. 1.

14. As was discussed in chapter one, military leaders feel very strongly that the position should be rotated. Many were upset at Taylor for breaking the pattern when he allowed himself to be recalled to active duty in 1962 to take over the chairmanship.

15. For comparability, table 11 compresses the Army's four levels into three by considering Corps and Army Command as the second level.

16. Janowitz, *Professional Soldier,* pp. 167–69.

CHAPTER THREE: THE BATTLE OF THE POTOMAC

Because the majority of the footnotes in this chapter will come from the annual congressional hearings on the defense budget, a simplified system to reduce the citations to manageable proportions has been used. References to the hearings of the committees will be found in the following form: HCA or HCAS, 1965, I, 57 and SCA, 1965, II 95. HCA and SCA refer to the House and Senate Appropriations Committees before which the hearings on the defense budget are conducted (HCAS = the House Armed Services Committee), the year refers to the fiscal year for which the money will be appropriated, and the roman numerals signify the volume number.

1. See Samuel Huntington, *The Common Defense* (New York: Columbia University, 1961); Warner Schilling et al, *Strategy Politics and Defense Budgets* (New York: Columbia University, 1962); and Demetrius Caraley, *The Politics of Military Unification* (New York: Columbia University, 1966).

2. Aaron Wildavsky, *The Politics of the Budgetary Process* (Boston: Little Brown, 1964).

3. Walter Millis, *The Forrestal Diaries* (New York: Viking, 1951), p. 475.

4. William Kaufmann, *The McNamara Strategy* (New York: Harper, 1964), p. 169.

5. HCA, 1949, III, 14.

6. SCA, 1965, I, 532.

7. Arthur Smithies, *The Budgetary Process of the United States* (New York: McGraw-Hill, 1955), pp. 9–10.

8. Bernard Gordon, "The Military Budget: Congressional Phase," *The Journal of Politics,* November 1961.

9. Millis, *Forrestal Diaries,* p. 415, and SCA, 1950, 17.

10. Millis, *Forrestal Diaries,* pp. 418 and 500.

11. Millis, *Forrestal Diaries,* p. 448.

12. Interview.

13. Millis, pp. 430 and 545.

14. HCA, 1950, I, 210–11.

15. HCA, 1950, IV, 567–75.

16. HCA, 1950, II, 439.

17. SCA, 1950, 32.

18. HCA, 1951, I, 104–106, 265–266.

19. SCA. 1951. 15. 16. 73 and HCA. 1951. II. 249.

20. This summary of the "revolt of the admirals" is primarily based upon Paul Hammond, "Supercarriers and B-36 Bombers," in *American Civil-Military Decisions* (Tuscaloosa: University of Alabama Press, 1963).

21. HCA, 1953, I, 57, 87–90, 97, 110–111, 142–145, and SCA 1953, 1, 5, 145–151.

22. *New York Times,* April 17, 1951, p. 4.

23. The components of the "Great Equation" were military and economic strength. The administration viewed the budgetary process as an exercise in balancing this equation, i.e., equating needed military strength with maximum economic strength. Eisenhower assumed that maximum economic strength rested on the foundation of a balanced budget.

24. The format for Eisenhower's budget was obtained from interviews, and Maxwell Taylor, *The Uncertain Trumpet* (New York: Harper, 1959), and Matthew Ridgway, *Soldier* (New York: Harper, 1956).

25. Taylor, pp. 82–83.

26. Alain Enthoven and K. Wayne Smith, *How Much is Enough* (New York: Harper, 1971), pp. 12–13.

27. Taylor, *Trumpet,* p. 206.

28. Interview.

29. Congress was dismayed when Eisenhower's FY 1959 budget, submitted about three months after Sputnik, amounted to only $37 billion. HCA, 1959, 353.

30. HCA, 1964, II, 585.

31. HCA, 1954, 317, 470–71, and HCA, 1955, 43–45. Wilson and Radford tried to convince the JCS that a sound economy was an aspect of national security and a proper subject for military appraisal.

32. Nathan Twining, *Neither Liberty nor Safety* (New York: Holt, Rhinehart and Winston, 1966), p. 56.

33. Taylor, *Trumpet,* p. 78.

34. Senate Preparedness Investigating Subcommittee, *Hearings on Major Defense Matters,* 86/1, May 20, 1959, p. 206, and interview.

35. Ridgway, *Soldier,* p. 102.

36. HCA, 1955, 43–45.

37. HCA, 1957, 432–558.

38. HCA, 1957, 737–40, 767, and SCA, 1957, 1221–50.

39. Carl Borklund, *Men of the Pentagon* (New York: Praeger,

1966), pp. 201–202, James Roherty, *Decisions of Robert McNamara* (Coral Gables: University of Miami Press, 1970), pp. 40–46.

40. HCA, 1963, 4.

41. The best source on McNamara's methods is Enthoven and Smith, *How Much is Enough?* The format for McNamara's budget procedures is adopted primarily from this book. I also relied on interviews. John Crecine, *Defense Budgeting* (Santa Monica: The Rand Corporation, 1970), and William Kaufmann, *The McNamara Strategy* (New York: Harper 1964), are also excellent sources.

42. HCA, 1963, II, 4–6.

43. Enthoven and Smith, *How Much,* p. 32.

44. Interview.

45. Enthoven and Smith, *How Much,* p. 94, call the JSOP the "best example of the unrealistic alternatives provided by the military." Enthoven's office wrote the MPM. See also Laurence Legere, "External Relations of the Department of Defense in the National Security Process," *Institute for Defense Analysis,* February 1970, p. 21.

46. HCA, 1968, I, 88. William Niskanen, "The Defense Resources Allocation Process," *Defense Management,* edited by Stephen Enke (Englewood Cliffs: Prentice Hall, 1967), p. 10. The PCRs would have added about $40 billion annually.

47. Enthoven and Smith, p. 56.

48. Crecine, p. 41.

49. Interviews.

50. Interview.

51. HCA, 1963, II, 4–6 and HCA, 1965, I, 304.

52. Roherty, p. 76.

53. HCA, 1967, I, 280; SCA, 1967, I, 69.

54. Townsend Hoopes, *The Limits of Intervention* (New York: David McKay, 1969), p. 90, and Philip Goulding, *Confirm or Deny* (New York: Harper, 1970), pp. 168–214.

55. Crecine, p. 51.

56. HCA, 1965, IV, 447–95.

57. Robert McNamara, "McNamara Defines His Job," *New York Times Magazine,* April 26, 1964, p. 108.

58. Thomas White, "Strategy and Defense Intellectuals," *Saturday Evening Post,* May 4, 1963, p. 10.

59. Curtis Lemay, *"America is in Danger,"* New York, Funk and Wagnalls, 1968, pp. viii to x.

60. HCA, 1969, I, 54–55.

61. George Anderson, "Address to the National Press Club," Washington, D.C., September 4, 1963.

62. His ideas on this subject are set down in a memorandum from Cyrus Vance, his deputy. It is printed in full in SCA, 1966, 285.

63. HCAS, 1966, 1331; SCA, 1966, I, 791; and HCA, 1966, III, 381.

64. HCA, 1968, II, 201, 723, 896–99.

65. Congress slashed about $7 billion from the last two budgets presented by the Johnson administration.

66. HCA, 1971, I, 153 and Enthoven and Smith, p. 334.

67. For a complete listing of the NSSMs through 1971, see John P. Leacacos, "Kissinger's Apparat," *Foreign Policy*, Winter 1971–72, pp. 25–27.

68. Laird's budget procedures are outlined in HCA, 1971, III, 480–81.

69. From FY 1970 through FY 1974, the services received $342.3 billion. The Army was given $111.5 billion or 32 percent, the Navy $120.7 billion or 34 percent, and the Air Force $120.1 billion or 34 percent.

70. Richard Nixon, *A New Strategy for Peace*, February 8, 1970, p. 20 and *Building for Peace*, February 25, 1971, p. 228.

71. Interviews.

72. Data furnished by the office of the Assistant Secretary of Defense, Comptroller.

73. For a complete analysis of the real impact of Congress, see my "Congressional Impact Upon the Defense Budget from 1962 to 1973: The Fiscal and Programmatic Hypotheses," *Naval War College Review*, November–December 1973, pp. 49–62.

74. Speech to the Armed Forces Management Association, Los Angeles, California, August 20, 1970.

CHAPTER FOUR: THE OPERATIONAL ROLE

1. The ambiguities of the chain of command were highlighted during the last days of the Nixon administration. According to press reports, Secretary of Defense Schlesinger directed the operational commanders not to carry out orders which came from the White House or elsewhere outside the normal military channels, that is, orders bypassing the Secretary of Defense and the JCS. It is the opinion of this author that it is perfectly legal for the President, as Commander-in-

Chief, to issue orders directly to operational commanders and in fact this has occurred repeatedly. For example, during the Vietnam peace negotiations, President Nixon bypassed normal lines of command to pass orders directly to the JCS for bombing strikes. The President did this because Secretary Laird was opposed to the bombing.

2. Lyndon Johnson, *The Vantage Point* (New York: Holt, Rhinehart, and Winston, 1971), p. 199.

3. Roger Hilsman, *To Move a Nation* (Garden City: Doubleday, 1964), p. 205.

4. Hilsman, *Nation,* p. 31 and Stuart Loory, *Defeated* (New York: Random House, 1973), p. 103.

5. James Clotfelter, *The Military in American Politics* (New York: Harper and Row, 1973), p. 215, and Lloyd Norman, "The Chiefs," Part II, *Army,* May 1970, pp. 37–43.

6. Hilsman, *Nation,* p. 129; Clotfelter, *The Military,* p. 217; and Matthew Ridgway, *Soldier* (New York: Harper, 1956), pp. 276–277.

7. This section relies heavily on the following excellent studies of the Korean conflict: Glenn Paige, *The Korean Decision* (New York: The Free Press, 1968); John Spanier, *Truman-MacArthur and the Korean War* (New York: Norton, 1965); Dean Acheson, *The Korean War* (New York: Norton, 1971); Matthew Ridgway, *The Korean War* (New York: Doubleday, 1967); and Richard Neustadt, *Presidential Power* (New York: Wiley, 1960).

8. Harry Truman, *Years of Trial and Hope* (New York: Doubleday, 1956), pp. 325–326.

9. Senate Armed Services and Foreign Relations Committees, *Hearings on the Military Situation in the Far East,* Washington, Government Printing Office, 1951, Part II, p. 753.

10. Hearings, Part IV, p. 2584.

11. Hearings, Part II, pp. 896, 942, 971.

12. Hearings, Part II, p. 1504.

13. Hearings, Part II, p. 1225.

14. Hearings, Part II, p. 1650.

15. Truman, *Trial and Hope,* p. 343.

16. Acheson, *Korean War,* p. 33. Bradley and Senate Majority Leader Scott Lucas (D-Ill) were the spokesmen for the anti-Smith view.

17. Ridgway, *Korean War,* p. 33.

18. Bradley received his fifth star and General of the Army rank one week after the Inchon landing.

19. For an excellent analysis of the interpersonal context of the time see John Lovell, *Foreign Policy in Perspective* (New York: Holt, Rhinehart, and Winston, 1970), pp. 48–53.

20. *New York Times,* June 29, 1950, p. 28.

21. Ridgway, *The Korean War,* pp. 38 and 39, and Douglas MacArthur, *Reminiscences* (New York: McGraw-Hill, 1964), pp. 346–52.

22. Acheson, *Korean War,* pp. 55–56.

23. Acheson, *Korean War,* p. 57.

24. MacArthur, *Reminiscences,* p. 362; Truman, *Trial and Hope,* p. 359; and Hearings, Part II, p. 718.

25. Ridgway, *The Korean War,* pp. 61–62.

26. Hearings, Part II, pp. 1229–1230; and Ridgway, p. 77.

27. Ridgway, *The Korean War,* p. 91.

28. Hearings, Part II, pp. 324, 331–332, 735–738.

29. The military arguments of the JCS against MacArthur's position were presented in the Senate Hearings and are well summarized by John Spanier, *Truman-MacArthur and the Korean War* (New York: Norton, 1965), pp. 240–246.

30. Ridgway, *The Korean War,* p. 154.

31. Acheson, *Korean War,* p. 105.

32. Ridgway, *The Korean War,* p. 62.

33. JCS memorandum on "United States Objectives and Courses of Action with Respect to Communist Aggression in Southeast Asia," *United States–Vietnam Relations,* VIII, p. 488.

34. Cablegram from Douglas Dillon, United States Ambassador to France, to Secretary of State John Foster Dulles, April 5, 1954. Neil Sheehan, Hedrick Smith, E. W. Kenworthy, and Fox Butterfield, *The Pentagon Papers: The Secret History of the Vietnam War as published by the New York Times* (New York: Bantam Books, 1971), p. 38 (hereafter referred to as *The Pentagon Papers*).

35. JCS Memorandum on "Studies with Respect to Possible U.S. Action Regarding Indochina," May 26, 1954, *The Pentagon Papers,* p. 44.

36. Ridgway, *Soldier,* pp. 276–277.

37. *The Pentagon Papers,* pp. 44–45.

38. *The Pentagon Papers,* pp. 14–15.

39. JCS Memorandum on "U.S. Forces in South Vietnam," May 10, 1961, *The Pentagon Papers,* p. 125.

40. *The Pentagon Papers,* p. 84.

41. Commander-in-Chief of the Pacific, a unified commander.
42. *The Pentagon Papers,* p. 97.
43. Maxwell Taylor, *Swords and Plowshares* (New York: Norton, 1972), pp. 242–244.
44. *The Pentagon Papers,* p. 105.
45. JCS Memorandum, "Urging a Greater Role in Vietnam," January 13, 1962, *The Pentagon Papers,* pp. 153–154.
46. Taylor, *Swords,* p. 288.
47. David Halberstam, *The Best and the Brightest* (New York: Random House, 1972), p. 204.
48. Taylor, *Swords,* p. 294.
49. JCS Memorandum on "Vietnam and Southeast Asia," January 22, 1964, *The Pentagon Papers,* p. 274.
50. *The Pentagon Papers,* pp. 247–251.
51. Taylor, *Swords,* p. 312.
52. *The Pentagon Papers,* p. 90.
53. *The Pentagon Papers,* pp. 260–263.
54. JCS Memorandum on "Recommended Courses of Action—Southeast Asia," August 26, 1964, *The Pentagon Papers,* pp. 354–355.
55. *The Pentagon Papers,* pp. 298–300, 312, 313.
56. *The Pentagon Papers,* pp. 308, 320, 338.
57. *The Pentagon Papers,* pp. 396–398.
58. *The Pentagon Papers,* p. 398.
59. *The Pentagon Papers,* pp. 397–399.
60. Cable from Ambassador Taylor to Secretary of State Dean Rusk, April 4, 1965, *The Pentagon Papers,* pp. 401–402.
61. *The Pentagon Papers,* pp. 402–405.
62. *The Pentagon Papers,* p. 413.
63. *The Pentagon Papers,* pp. 462–464.
64. Interviews.
65. *The Pentagon Papers,* pp. 462–465.
66. Halberstam, *Best and Brightest,* p. 595.
67. Department of Defense Report to the Senate Armed Services Committee, September 10, 1973 (hereafter referred to as DOD White Paper).
68. Henry Trewhitt, *McNamara* (New York: Harper and Row, 1971), p. 225.
69. *The Pentagon Papers,* pp. 462–470.
70. *The Pentagon Papers,* pp. 475–481, 511, 515.

71. *The Pentagon Papers,* pp. 589–595. Marvin Kalb and Elie Abel, *The Roots of Involvement* (New York: Norton, 1971), also discuss the post-Tet activities of the JCS.

72. "Report of the Chairman, JCS, On the Situation in Vietnam and MACV Requirements," February 27, 1968. *The Pentagon Papers,* pp. 615–621.

73. For a complete account of this bureaucratic struggle see the following: *The Pentagon Papers,* pp. 600–612; Clark Clifford, "A Vietnam Appraisal," *Foreign Affairs,* July 1969, pp. 601–622; Lyndon Johnson, *The Vantage Point* (New York: Holt, Rhinehart and Winston, 1971), pp. 380–424; Townsend Hoopes, *The Limits of Intervention* (New York: David McKay, 1969), pp. 139–224; and Taylor, *Swords,* pp. 381–391.

74. Clifford, "A Vietnam Appraisal," p. 615.

75. DOD White Paper.

76. Letter from Lieutenant General John Lavelle to Senator John Stennis, dated September 26, 1972; excerpts are printed in the *New York Times,* October 6, 1972.

77. At the same time that Lavelle was defying the ground rules, President Nixon was ordering secret bombings of North Vietnam to "emphasize" the discussions that Henry Kissinger was conducting with the North Vietnamese. This information is contained in a brief filed by attorneys for John Erlichman on June 20, 1974, with U.S. District Judge Gerhard Gesell.

78. For an excellent analysis of the Abrams' strategy, see Maynard Parker, "Vietnam: The War That Won't End," *Foreign Affairs,* January 1975, pp. 352–361. This account is adopted from Parker's perceptive article.

79. For an excellent account of the JCS attitude on the air war, see "The Briefing by Admiral Thomas Moorer of Newsmen on January 9, 1973," *Washington Post,* January 10, 1972, A10:1.

80. See Leslie Gelb, "Vietnam: The System Worked," *Foreign Policy,* Summer 1971, pp. 140–173, for a discussion of this point. Gelb also notes that scholars and journalists shared these assumptions.

CHAPTER FIVE: CONCLUSION

1. In his farewell speech on July 2, 1974, Admiral Moorer remarked, ". . . one day I read that the Joint Chiefs are weak and never consulted, and another day that they are controlling the country. . . ."

2. Halberstam, *Best and Brightest,* p. 564.

3. Defense spending accounts for about 70 percent of the controllable expenditures in the federal budget. Joint Committee on Reduction of Federal Expenditures, *Staff Report No. 11,* pp. 14 and 41.

4. Pete Glazer, "Army's Drug Use in Europe Still a Problem, Official Says," *Navy Times,* May 22, 1974, p. 35.

5. David Kelly, "Must the Marine Corps Shrink or Die?" *Armed Forces Journal,* October 1974, pp. 18–20.

6. Department of Defense survey cited by Marine Major General Norman Gourley in a speech to an American Legion group in September 1974.

7. Senate Armed Services Committee Report, December 21, 1974.

8. Interview with Admiral James Holloway, *Navy Times,* September 25, 1974, pp. 1 and 48.

9. William Chapman, "Military Most Admired U.S. Institution," *Washington Post,* May 9, 1974, p. 1.

10. For example, reservists have recently taken over a substantial portion of the refueling mission of strategic aircraft.

Index

Collins, Joseph L.—(cont.)
54; and Korean War, 137–38, 143, 146, 147; table 1, 2, 3, 4, 5
Combined Chiefs of Staff, 14
Congress: Senate approval of appointments to JCS, 6–7, 194n6; advised by JCS, 7, 9–11, 95, 109, 120; budget hearings, 99–103, 108–9, 127, 130, 198n29; cuts defense spending, 181–82, 200n65
Connally, John B., 4, 35, 60, 194n5
Cowan, James R., 183
Cuban missile crisis, 61, 134

Dawkins, Peter, col., 34
Decker, George H., gen.: 34, 191; background and career, 41–42, 47, 51, 53, 54; table 1, 2, 3, 4, 5
Defense, Department of: 18; organization, 5, 13, 16, 104, 111–12; costs, 182–83, 186, 190; table 12, 13
Defense, Secretary of: 8, 12, 18–19, 27; advised by JCS, 7, 9–11, 16, 132; attends JCS meetings, 9, 21; military chain of command, 11–12, 132, 200n1; selects some JCS members, 33–34; table 12, 13. See also Clifford; Forrestal; Gates; Johnson; Laird; Lovett; McElroy; McNamara; Marshall; Wilson
defense budget: 9, 18; and Congress, 99–103, 108–9, 111, 119–21, 127–28, 130–31, 181–82; and military policy, 95–96; during Truman administration, 96–103; during Eisenhower administration, 104–11; during Kennedy and Johnson administrations, 111–21; during Nixon administration, 121–28; JCS role summarized, 128–31
Defense Program Review Committee, 124, 126
defense spending, 181–83, 215n3, table 12
defense superagencies, 5n, 12, 13, 17, fig. 1
Denfield, Louis E., adm.: 99; and supercarrier United States, 19, 68, 85, 101–2; background and career, 54–56, 64, 69, 71; table 6, 7
Diem, Ngo Dinh, 150–51, 152, 154–55
Dominican Republic, U.S. troops to, 133–34, 135

domino theory, 151, 164, 176
Dulles, John F., 9, 149

Eisenhower, Dwight D.: 11, 111; appointments to JCS, 6, 30–32, 35–36, 86; defense budgets, 104–11, 128; view of JCS role in budget process, 107–8, 109–10; massive retaliation strategy, 108; table 3

F-111 fighter plane, 61, 68
Fechteler, William M., adm., 57, 68, 69, 71, table 6, 7
Felt, Harry D., adm., 152, 153
Five-Year Defense Plan, 112–13, 122, 124, 125
flexible response strategy, 24, 32, 108
Ford, Gerald R., 9, 190
Forrestal, James V.: 18, 27; and defense budgets, 95, 97–99
Friedheim, Jerry W., 33–34

Gates, Thomas S., 21, 110–11
Geneva Accords, 1954, 150–51
Gilpatric, Roswell L., 152
Goodpaster, Andrew J., gen., 34
Gordon, Bernard K., 95
"Great Equation" budget formula, 104, 198n23

Haig, Alexander M., gen., 32
Harkins, Paul D., gen., 21, 153, 154
Harriman, W. Averell, 143, 154
Helms, Richard M., 161
Hilsman, Roger, 154
Holloway, James L., 64, 188
Hoover Commission, 1947–49, 18, 133

Inchon landing, 139–40, 142–43

Janowitz, Morris, 30, 91
Johnson, Harold K., gen.: 35, 50, 172; background and career, 43–44, 47, 51, 53, 88, 161, 194n14; table 1, 2, 3, 4, 5
Johnson, Louis A., 99–102, 137
Johnson, Lyndon B.: 7, 25, 109, 130; appointees to JCS, 6, 30–31, 36, 62, 77, 86; budget review, 9, 118; and McNamara, 117, 120; and Vietnam War, 10, 132, 155–56, 159–66; table 3